Coping with Heart Surgery and Bypassing Depression

Coping with Heart Surgery and Bypassing Depression:

A Family's Guide to the Medical, Emotional, and Practical Issues

Carol Cohan, M.A.
June B. Pimm, Ph.D.
James R. Jude, M.D.

PSYCHOSOCIAL PRESS

The following publishers have generously given permission to use extended quotations from copyrighted works: From "How to Have Open-Heart Surgery (and Almost Love It)," by Douglass Cater, in *The New York Magazine,* 5/14/78. Copyright © 1978 by The New York Times Company. Reprinted by permission. From *Helping Cardiac Patients: Behavioral and Psychotherapeutic Approaches,* by Andrew M. Razin and Associates. Copyright © 1985 by Jossey-Bass, Inc., Publishers. Reprinted by permission. From *Heartsounds,* by Martha Weinman Lear. Copyright © 1980 by Martha Weinman Lear. Reprinted by permission of Simon & Schuster, Inc. From *The Psychological Experience of Surgery,* by Richard Blacher, editor. Copyright © 1987 by Wiley-Interscience, a subsidiary of John Wiley & Sons. Reprinted by permission.

Library of Congress Cataloging-in-Publication Data

Cohan, Carol, 1943-
    Coping with heart surgery and bypassing depression : a family's
guide to the medical, emotional, and practical issues / Carol Cohan,
June B. Pimm, James R. Jude.
      p.   cm.
    Rev. ed. of: A patient's guide to heart surgery. 1991.
    Includes index.
    ISBN 1-887841-07-5 (pbk.)
    1. Coronary artery bypass—Popular works. 2. Coronary artery
bypass—Psychological aspects. 3. Depression, Mental—Prevention.
I. Pimm, June B., 1927-   . II. Jude, James R.   III. Cohan, Carol.
1943-   Patient's guide to heart surgery. IV. Title.
RD598.35.C67C65 1997
617.4'12—dc21   97-21699
                                                          CIP

Manufactured in the United States of America

In Memory of Michael A. Lipsky
A Casualty of Innocence

TABLE OF CONTENTS

FOREWORD

As a practicing cardiologist over the past 25 years, I have been struck by the number of patients, friends, and acquaintances who have complained to me about how inadequately they were prepared to meet the psychological stress of heart surgery.

In today's world of multispecialty team medicine, failure of communication is an increasing problem, and although many patients are satisfied with a photocopied instruction sheet and a hasty viewing of a video, many expect a deeper and more thorough understanding of their apprehension and a fuller explanation of the strange new world that they are about to encounter.

Coping with Heart Surgery and Bypassing Depression is the answer to their prayers (and mine). In this book, the authors take the prospective patient step-by-step through the surgical process from diagnosis to the resumption of activities and a return to the workplace. Their years of experience in researching hundreds of patients undergoing cardiac surgery place them in a unique position to provide the most appropriate information, advice, and encouragement to candidates for heart surgery. Chapter by chapter, in the most knowledgeable and reassuring manner, the prospective patient is led through the events he or she will experience. The purpose of this book is to minimize the risk of anxiety, frustration, and depression during the period surrounding the operation that is so often the cause of delayed recovery, increased risk of complications, and reduced surgical benefit.

For the discerning patient about to undergo heart surgery, as well as his loved ones, this book will be like a trusted companion and knowledgeable adviser, and, in my opinion, it should never be far from the bedside.

R. F. P. Cronin,
FRCP (London), FRCP (Canada)
Former Director, Canadian Heart Association
Former Dean, Faculty of Medicine, McGill University

A NOTE FROM THE AUTHORS

Carol Cohan, M.A., first became involved with the Miami study that inspired this text as a medical writer in 1984. James Jude, M.D., served as medical consultant during the original research and as a guiding spirit for this book. June Pimm, Ph.D., together with Joseph Feist, Ph.D., designed and led the study. Thus, the first person is used in the ensuing pages with editorial license.

Except for people whose experiences have previously been published, patients' names and other identifying features have been changed to protect their privacy.

Since the English language offers no gender-free singular pronoun applicable to people, we were hard put to avoid sex bias in this text without sacrificing fluidity of style. We fully recognize that physicians, nurses, other professionals, spouses, and patients come in both male and female form, and we hope that, in an attempt to achieve readability, we have not implied otherwise.

ACKNOWLEDGMENTS

This book would not have been possible without the support of the American Heart Association, Miami Chapter, which provided funds for our research on depression and coronary bypass surgery.

Abundant thanks go to the physicians who generously participated in this project: Drs. Richard P. Cohen, Paul DeWitt, Malcolm Dorman, Thomas Gentsch, Charles Hyams, Parry B. Larson, Susan Light, John Lister, Norton Luger, James Margolis, Jerry Stolzenberg, Ernest Traad, and Jonathan Tuerk. We are also grateful to Jeff Raines, Ph.D.; Andrea Fisch, R.N., M.P.H.; Shirley Haskell and Memorial Hospital's chapter of Mended Hearts; Sally Kolitz, Ph.D.; Ronni Korschun, R.D., M.S.; Patti Perlman, Psy. D.; Paul Stickney; Libby Strauss; and Judith Wolfe, M.S.W. Thanks, too, to the scores of patients who shared their confidences so that future patients and their families might benefit. Our deepest gratitude goes to Catherine Tuerk, M.A., R.N., C.S., a wise and sensitive psychotherapist.

Much of the research for this book took place at North Ridge Medical Center/Heart Institute in Fort Lauderdale, Florida, and never could have been accomplished without the enthusiastic assistance of the fine, caring professional staff. Most of all, thank you to Barbara Friedman, R.N., M.S. In addition, we also thank Karen Baumann, P.A.-C.; Carol Dwyer, R.N., M.S.N.; Ali Ghahramani, M.D.; Sue Jones, R.P.T.; Richard Monti, P.A.-C.; Stuart Nesbitt, P.A.-C.; Cindy Porter, R.N.; Shari Scrop, R.D.; David Stahler, P.A.-C.; Alan Stillerman, R.T.; and Margo Snedden.

We are indebted to Bess Marder and Robert Pimm for their editorial talents. Thanks also to Raymond Marat, and Joseph R. Feist, Ph.D., for their contributions to this manuscript. Finally, we appreciate the commitment of The Pickering Press, which first published this book; Susan Randol, who demonstrated tremendous enthusiasm for this project; Cynthia Barrett and Carol Cohen, our editors at HarperCollins, publishers of the second edition; and Margaret Emery, Ph.D., and her dedicated staff at Psychosocial Press.

INTRODUCTION TO THE
THIRD EDITION

Coping with Heart Surgery and Bypassing Depression is the third incarnation of this book, which was first published as *The Heart Surgery Handbook* (The Pickering Press, 1988) and then as *A Patient's Guide to Heart Surgery* (HarperCollins, 1991). Over the years, an ever-growing body of research has strengthened our original position and confirmed the validity of our work, and we have incorporated the new research into this updated text. This revision also reflects the reality that hospital stays are shorter than they used to be, thanks to improved technology and better care, as well as efforts to contain costs. Since angioplasty has become increasingly viable, we have enlarged our discussion of that alternative to bypass, and we have added a brief mention of the new "Band-Aid bypass" procedure. Finally, we have amplified our attention to strategies aimed at arresting heart disease, and we have updated our resources to reflect the best of newly published material.

We bring you *Coping with Heart Surgery and Bypassing Depression* knowing it can help you get well. Arrogant though this claim may sound, we make it with confidence because we saw how well the first edition of this text performed in a study that measured the effectiveness of various patient education efforts. The key, we believe, is our unique combination of practical information and solutions to common problems. In addition, patients have reported that the volume is easy to use and that it helped their families to support them in a meaningful way.

While this book is unquestionably about heart surgery, much of the information it contains is not unique to this experience. Many of its theories and strategies also pertain to recuperation from heart attack, other debilitating illnesses, and other kinds of surgery. Thus, we believe *Coping with Heart Surgery and Bypassing Depression* has application to a broad range of health crises. These claims are based on numerous studies which demonstrate that, regardless of the medical predicament, when patients understand their problems and have ready strategies for coping with them, they recover more quickly. Heart attack patients, for example, recovered with marked speed when they received a short course in coronary heart disease and its treatment in addition to standard information. They responded well to watching their electrocardiogram (EKG) tracings and exercising under supervision. Similarly, patients scheduled for abdominal surgery benefited from learning what to expect after surgery, how to relax by deep breathing, and how to protect their incisions when they moved. These patients left the hospital sooner and needed less pain medication than those given standard patient education. Women undergoing hysterectomy also confirmed the principle. With information designed to quiet preoperative fear and help them manage postoperative pain, they suffered less anxiety, as measured by lowered blood pressure and heart rate. It is this theory, too, which is responsible for the proliferation of childbirth classes; understanding labor and delivery and practicing exercises to cope with the process have enabled countless women to suffer less pain and need less medication than they otherwise would. All these studies document that convalescents benefit from appropriate attention to their emotional concerns.

Features of this Text

In *Coping with Heart Surgery and Bypassing Depression* we provide detailed information about the events that accompany each stage of the heart surgery experience, from the time surgery is recommended until months after convalescence is under way. We discuss what other patients encountered at each stage, problems that arose, and solutions that worked for a variety of people with different personalities and coping styles. While this text touches on heart disease and its treatment alternatives, it is primarily designed as a coping tool. If you know what to expect, if you can perceive your problems as normal, and if you can identify solutions that seem appropriate for you, the problems become less threatening. Put another way, knowing what to expect makes the unknown more manageable.

Most people who have had heart surgery agree it is important to know exactly what to expect every step of the way. Moreover, their experiences suggest that when they have time to assimilate the information slowly, they process it more effectively and can call upon it more reliably than when they are bombarded with it immediately before surgery. Several people who had to undergo emergency bypass and were given all their instructions in the minutes before they were put to sleep, experienced panic when they woke up, whereas those who had time to prepare had a greater sense of calm and control.

Mental Health and Physical Recovery

Coping with Heart Surgery and Bypassing Depression is our latest attempt to alleviate the severe depression that can impede recovery from heart surgery. As more than 50 studies have documented, this depression afflicts up to one-third of all heart surgery patients in the weeks and months following their operations. Worse, because of the unique nature of heart surgery, this condition is often masked. Instead of feeling despondent, people suffering postsurgical depression commonly experience poor appetite; difficulty sleeping; lethargy; trouble with thinking, concentrating, and remembering; and an assortment of physical ailments that elude diagnosis. Yet these problems are real, and they interfere with resuming work and leisure activities.

Our efforts to ease these difficulties began in 1979 with a 3-year study to test the merits of supportive counseling for coronary bypass patients. By 1982, we had shown that counseling instituted before surgery and sustained for 3 months afterward was instrumental in reducing debilitating depression. In this study, which is described fully in chapter 1, patients who received counseling experienced less post-surgical depression and fewer medical problems than those who received standard patient education. Consequently, those who had counseling were able to recapture a sense of wellness and vigor more quickly than those who did not.

Counseling designed to allay anxiety and solve problems appears to be critically important to patients with heart disease. This theme also emerges in research by Nancy Frasure-Smith, Ph.D., at McGill University. In this study, nurses telephoned men recovering from heart attacks once a month to monitor their stress. If someone seemed distressed or if he had been rehospitalized, he was visited by a nurse specializing in heart disease. She short-circuited his apprehension by meeting his needs at the moment. In an average of 5 to 6 hours of private counseling over a year's time, nurses provided information about chest pain, shortness of breath, fatigue, depression, anxiety, and medication. They also rendered emotional support and made referrals to health care professionals. This program cut the death rate in half during the year the study was in progress. Four years later, the numbers continued to persuade the researchers that alleviating stress can save lives.

In follow-up research, presented at the 67th annual scientific sessions of the American Heart Association in November 1994, Dr. Fraser-Smith demonstrated that depression after a heart attack makes patients vulnerable to a potentially fatal form of abnormal heart rhythm. Her data indicate that depression can threaten survival after heart attacks for up to 18 months. Also reporting at this conference, Johns Hopkins epidemiologist Daniel E. Ford, M.D., found a correlation between depression and heart attacks among more than 1,000 people followed for 35 years. Together these studies strengthen the growing belief that, left untreated, depression makes people vulnerable to heart disease and premature death.

Dr. Frasure-Smith's work showed that simple, inexpensive intervention can protect health as successfully as more costly elaborate approaches. The essential ingredient, apparently, is a cushion of support during the months when patients feel most vulnerable and find coping particularly difficult. The notion that a simple approach is sufficient appeared in our research, too. Effective though our counseling was, our results suggested that, in perhaps two-thirds of cases, more modest intervention would have worked just as well. So we set out to achieve the outcome of counseling in a less expensive, less cumbersome way. The result was *The Heart Surgery Handbook*, the first incarnation of this book. It was designed specifically to provide the kind of medical information, problem-solving strategies, and emotional support that counselors gave to patients and their families in our study.

A Book as Counselor

To test the effectiveness of the book, we evaluated how well it controlled depression compared to the counseling offered during our original study, to tapes and pamphlets designed to achieve the same purpose, and to standard patient education. It is the outcome of this research, alluded to at the beginning of this introduction, that makes us confident that *Coping with Heart Surgery and Bypassing Depression* can ease recovery. Twelve weeks after surgery, patients who received standard patient education experienced depression at an alarming rate of 24%. The specially designed books and tapes brought that rate down a notch to 19%. Counseling had better results: 14%. Surprisingly, the book worked best of all, reducing depression to just 7%.

Perhaps patients who received the book encountered so little depression because they used it so diligently. Three-quarters of the patients and almost all their spouses read the book; two-thirds of the patients said they continued to refer to it during convalescence, which was not the case with the pamphlets and tapes. While just about the same percentage of patients used these other materials initially, only half the spouses did, and barely a third of the patients continued to refer to their aids during convalescence.

Apparently, families also played a crucial role. According to the observations of hospital personnel, when patients had read the book, their spouses and children appeared noticeably free from anxiety, presumably because the book answered their questions and quieted their fears. The patients undoubtedly sensed their families' ease and felt reassured by it. In addition, the book enabled families to support patients by reminding them of relevant information and making helpful suggestions as the need arose. The book thus equipped the families to be effective supporters.

The Importance of Social Support

Though we cannot prove it, we sense a strong connection linking the presence of close family, the fact that the family members used the book, and the strikingly low rate of depression among these patients. We think the book helped the families to help the patients keep depression at bay. Our suspicion gained confirmation with several studies reported in recent years. A 1993 report from Sweden showed that lack of social support stood as a separate risk factor for heart disease. In 1994, a project that looked specifically at how social support affected the recovery of elderly patients found that this kind of help, especially from family, could promote recovery when support is constructive but that it can hinder recovery if the support is negative. On a similar note, another 1993 report suggested that social support is most effective in improving recovery from bypass surgery when it enhances self-esteem, possibly because when people feel good about themselves they can cope more successfully.

The contrasting experiences of participants in our latest study suggest that knowledgeable allies can be indispensable to heart surgery patients. This notion concurs with the

growing evidence that social support can alleviate stress.
Most recently, Dr. Seymour Levine, a neuroimmunologist
at Stanford University, showed how feelings of uncertainty
can trigger a rise in stress hormones in laboratory animals.
He also demonstrated that the presence of a familiar animal
can dilute the negative impact of this uncertainty. In hu-
mans, he suspects, the presence of supporters achieves the
same results. Similarly, our findings suggest that *Coping
with Heart Surgery and Bypassing Depression* can bring a
measure of security and comfort to this difficult experience
and that the key members of a support system are the avenue
through which this reassurance is conveyed.

We were surprised to discover just how profound the
role of supporter is. When we wrote the first edition, we
intended it primarily for patients. We included chapter 8,
''When Someone You Love Has Heart Surgery,'' because
we felt that heart surgery is as much a crisis for mates and
children as it is for patients, but traditionally the families
are deprived of much needed assistance. Now, we realize,
this chapter is indirectly relevant to patients as well. What's
more, the rest of the book is as much a guide for loved ones
as it is for patients themselves.

When Women Need Surgery

Since the first edition of this book was published, the impact
of coronary heart disease on women has become the subject
of considerable attention and controversy. Perhaps the most
striking realization to emerge is that, although women are
nearly as vulnerable to coronary heart disease as men, the
medical profession is surprisingly ignorant about the particular ways of women's hearts. In the years to come, research
will close this gap. In the meantime, the subject deserves
some mention.

For women as well as men, the success rate for invasive
management of coronary artery disease is exceedingly high.
Among the tiny percentage who do not do well, more

women than men run into immediate trouble with angioplasty. This technique, commonly called the balloon procedure, is discussed in chapter 2 under "Deciding On Bypass." But women who survive angioplasty are more likely than men to enjoy long-lasting results. Similarly, fewer men die or suffer heart attacks soon after bypass. When women survive the immediate postoperative period, they live as long as their male counterparts; however, women, more than men, continue to experience chest pain and find their bypasses closing up. Although researchers are just now beginning to investigate why women have this problem, a number of theories have been put forth. Some experts attribute women's difficulties to the fact that they are smaller than men and have smaller coronary arteries. Others observe that women are significantly more likely to have diabetes and high blood pressure, both of which increase risk. Perhaps depression is a significant factor, since women tend to be more depressed than men immediately before and after surgery. We wonder to what extent social issues enter the picture. Women, much more than men, are likely to be widowed when they undergo surgery, and women receive less social support in general. Women's ability to recover well after surgery has also been correlated to their level of satisfaction with other aspects of their lives.

Increasingly, experts conjecture that women have more trouble because they are older and sicker when they enter surgery. Women, on average, develop coronary artery disease about 10 years later than men, a fact that explains why they have surgery at a more advanced age. As for why they go into surgery with more advanced heart disease, perhaps it is because they are more difficult to diagnose. Women often have inconsequential chest pains and irregular heartbeats, while the same symptoms in men usually mean trouble. Moreover, stress tests are notably less reliable in women than they are in men; sometimes the only way to confirm coronary artery disease in women is by catheterization, a procedure too invasive and expensive to be prescribed cavalierly. Finally, the pain caused by constricted coronary arteries, known as angina, is not followed by heart attacks in women as often as it is in men. This disparity once persuaded many medical practitioners that coronary artery disease did not threaten women. Justifiably, this view is changing.

After comparing the surgical experiences of men and women, some critics accuse the medical profession of holding a bias against women. While this belief is certainly not unanimous, it is probably safe to say that some cardiologists and heart surgeons are ignorant of and insensitive to the distinctive medical and psychological circumstances of female patients.

If you are a woman facing heart surgery, we urge you to choose physicians who are familiar with the unique dynamics of heart disease in females and feel comfortable relating to women. And if you are concerned that you face added surgical risk because of your sex, you might raise this issue with your physicians. If they believe that you are a good candidate, you have every reason to trust them, since most women come through surgery as successfully as men.

Male or female, young or old, if you are having surgery to treat coronary artery disease, you must be aware that surgery will not cure this disease. Rather, it is a stop-gap measure, a second chance for you to safeguard your health. Coronary heart disease is a progressive condition accelerated by numerous risk factors; some, including age, genetic predisposition, and male gender, are beyond anyone's control; others, such as high blood pressure, high cholesterol, obesity, diabetes, smoking, formation of blood clots, stress, sedentary life-style, we all have some power to control. Research shows that, by reducing these risk factors, it is possible to hold heart disease at bay. We encourage you to embrace this challenge because we want you to enjoy the benefits of your surgery for many years to come.

From the surgeon's perspective, heart surgery has become reassuringly routine and predictable. But from the patient's perspective, it is an exquisitely personal experience that no two people go into or emerge from in exactly the same way. More important, there is no right or wrong way to approach the procedure or manage recovery. When learning that he should have surgery, one patient headed straight for the golf course while another went to her safety deposit box to review her will. A third arranged a candlelight dinner with his wife, where they reflected upon the years when their marriage was young and their children were small.

By the same token, we encourage you to approach this book in whatever way feels right. Perhaps you feel compelled to go directly to the chapter on the intensive care unit. Perhaps you prefer to begin with the interconnection of mind and body, which is discussed in chapter 10. You may want to read from cover to cover or you may want to look for specific information. In using this book, as in undergoing surgery, you would do best to follow the course that feels most comfortable to you.

Chapter One

BYPASSING DEPRESSION

*If only I had known what to expect,
this would have been so much easier.*
—Common patient complaint

In 1967, when Drs. Rene C. Favaloro and Dudley Johnson developed coronary artery bypass graft surgery, the notion of surgically improving blood flow to the heart seemed a radical experiment. Within 15 years, however, more than a million such operations were performed, and now it is more common than any other major surgery. Today, there are more than 350,000 bypass operations a year in the United States alone, and for good reason. For the right patient, bypass surgery promises more years of active, high-quality life than any other treatment.

Although the idea of opening the chest and repairing the heart seems ominous, the surgery has a superb 97% success rate. Considering that many patients who undergo bypass surgery are 75, 80, 85 years old and suffer from chronic diseases characteristic of old age, this figure is indeed impressive. Among younger, otherwise healthy people, the statistics are even better.

Most patients recover without major incident. Within hours after surgery, they commonly show healthy color in their faces even though they are still asleep from anesthesia. Within a couple of days, most stroll the hospital corridors chatting with nurses and visitors. In less than 12 weeks, even some octogenarians are strong enough to walk outside when the weather is mild. This kind of dramatic progress is one factor that makes heart surgery so desirable. Ironically, this dramatic speed of recovery may cause problems for some patients.

Inured to a procedure that is usually uneventful, and reluctant to upset their patients with descriptions of postoperative difficulties, medical personnel sometimes imply that the operation is trifling and that recovery is easy. Thus, too many patients hear, "We'll just open your chest, fix your plumbing, and in six weeks, you'll be back on the golf course."

In light of the routine nature of most cases this attitude is understandable. But when you are contemplating surgery or when someone you love is being wheeled to the operating room, the event takes on more imposing proportions. Few people undergo surgery without facing their mortality head on. Beforehand, nearly all patients and their families feel anxious. Afterward, patients commonly endure pain and discomfort, lingering weakness, and periodic dejection. Most do not feel like themselves for months. When medical personnel underestimate these physical and emotional difficulties, patients sometimes have trouble reconciling the contradiction between what they hear and what they feel. When this happens, they can experience more physical and emotional pain and take longer to recover than those who know what to expect.

The Problem

One of the most common difficulties after surgery is depression. An early study of 34 patients at the University of North Carolina revealed that, although surgery was successful in all cases, 83% remained unemployed and 57% were sexually impotent up to 12 years later.

These patients reported limited activity, distorted body image, poor self-esteem, and lingering depression. The researchers of this study asserted that the psychological welfare and social adjustment of bypass patients demand more attention. To date, several dozen studies echo the conclusion that, while bypass does eradicate or diminish chest pain, many patients are unable to live the fulfilling lives they had anticipated.

As Jonathan Halperin, director of clinical cardiology at New York's Mount Sinai Medical Center, observed, "Patients are robbed of their sense of well-being or infused

"We'll just open your chest, fix your plumbing, and in six weeks, you'll be back on the golf course."

with self-doubt. Others cope with the realization of having suddenly grown frail and old. . . . This post-bypass syndrome is taking on the dimensions of a public health problem in its own right.''

The Study

Because this problem afflicts so many people, we devised a study to help us understand and solve it. We hypothesized that most patients who failed to feel well despite successful surgery were suffering from depression, and that if we could relieve their depression, they would recover more quickly and fully.

What followed was a 3-year project that assessed depression in bypass patients and evaluated the effectiveness of specific short-term supportive counseling in alleviating it.[1] The study, funded by the American Heart Association, confirmed that surgery leaves approximately one-third of patients depressed. At the 3-year mark, 28% of patients who received standard care developed such severe depression that it prevented them from feeling their surgery had been successful. However, when the psychological adjustment of patients and their families received special attention, they fared better. With supportive counseling, the incidence of depression dropped to 6% after 3 years. Most important of all, the study showed that patients who were likely to suffer from enduring depression shared certain characteristics, and therefore it was possible to predict which patients needed counseling most.

The Nature of Crisis and Crisis Intervention

The counseling that the Miami study set out to test follows the guidelines for crisis intervention devised by Gerald

[1]The results of this study were first published in *Psychological Risks of Coronary Bypass Surgery* by June B. Pimm, Ph.D. and Joseph R. Feist, Ph.D. (Plenum, 1984).

Caplan, formerly director of Harvard University Medical School's Laboratory of Community Psychiatry. This counseling is specifically designed to ease the psychological consequences of crisis. It is not psychotherapy, not analytical, and not intended to uncover secrets of the unconscious. Its sole purpose is to enable people to function effectively when they feel most vulnerable. In the face of earthquakes, violence of various kinds, and other catastrophes, psychologists often use crisis intervention to help people cope. We chose this kind of counseling because heart surgery poses many of the same challenges to coping as other kinds of crisis.

When coping becomes difficult, people stop functioning in their usual ways. They feel overwhelmed and anxious. And they have trouble solving problems and setting priorities. The havoc that results makes them feel helpless. With successful intervention, however, people in crisis learn to anticipate what will happen, understand how they normally cope with crises, and then mobilize those strategies. Counseling thus empowers people to overcome their feelings of vulnerability.

Coping styles vary from person to person, and there is no right or wrong style. For example, when a hurricane 500 miles off the coast of Florida seemed to be headed for Miami, Mildred Nerler scurried about bringing in all her potted plants and outdoor furniture. She wanted to be prepared for the worst. Her neighbor thought she was crazy and chose to sit tight until he heard a later forecast.

"Maybe I'll have to scramble at the last minute," he said, "but sure as heck I'm not going to drag all this stuff in for nothing."

Though coping styles are highly personal, everyone usually resorts to the same style time and again. Mrs. Nerler does her Christmas shopping in September; her neighbor never starts until the week before the holiday. Long before Mrs. Nerler goes on vacation, she begins laying out the clothes she will take. Carefully and unhurriedly, she packs her suitcase, making sure to have it closed and ready the night before her trip. Her neighbor doesn't even begin to think about what he'll take until the night before he leaves. Then, he throws whatever looks clean into a suitcase and hopes he's well prepared. Everyone's responses follow a predictable course, and in a catastrophe people fall back on the strategies they have always found most helpful.

Because people feel overwhelmed and anxious at these times, however, they often have trouble making even their most effective strategies work. One of the goals of counseling is to help people adapt their most reliable strategies to the demands of the trauma. Fortunately, people in crisis seem especially receptive to this therapy.

Method of the Miami Study

To test whether crisis intervention could help heart surgery patients, we chose 104 people of similar profile, divided them into two groups, and measured their levels of depression before surgery. Patients in both groups took a battery of nine self-administered psychological tests to measure their levels of depression as well as a number of personality dimensions. Several of these tools proved extremely helpful. To measure depression, we used the Beck Depression Inventory, which asks patients to endorse or reject statements like these: ''I feel bad or unworthy a good part of the time'' and ''I feel I am being punished.'' These items are intended to reveal the extent to which respondents have adopted a pessimistic attitude toward life. The Beck Depression Inventory measures the way people think and feel, including physical symptoms, since each of these factors can reflect depression.

Patients also responded to the Rotter Locus of Control Scale. This test reveals whether people believe they control their lives or whether they feel their lives are controlled by an outside force. People who, in Rotter's words, have an *internal locus of control* would affirm statements like ''for a well-prepared student there is rarely, if ever, an unfair test'' or ''becoming successful is a matter of hard work; luck has little or nothing to do with it.'' In contrast, those with an *external locus of control* would probably believe that ''without the right breaks, one cannot be an effective leader'' or ''che serà, serà.''

Another valuable measure was an adapted form of the Recent Life Changes Questionnaire. This tool, developed by psychiatrists Thomas Holmes and Richard Rahe, lists 100 common life occurrences, each with a point value corresponding to the intensity of its emotional impact. By indicating which events they had experienced within the preceding 6 months, respondents reveal how much they taxed their coping resources during that period.

During hospitalization, all patients received whatever counseling and support surgical patients normally receive at the two participating hospitals. In addition, patients in one group received the following assistance:

> Before surgery, our counselors told the patients and their families exactly what events would occur and what sensations and emotions they were likely to feel.

> After surgery, counselors gave patients and their families detailed information about the physical and emotional aspects of recovery as well as hospital routine.

> The counselors encouraged nurses, clergy, and family to be supportive.

> After discharge, a counselor visited each patient and his family at home once a week for 8 weeks, by which time the crisis presumably had ended and the patients and their families were functioning as usual. These visits were devoted largely to trying to help the family help the patient.

> The counselors offered specific suggestions for solving problems pertinent to surgery and recovery, but they

avoided becoming involved in extraneous problems, such as stressful family relationships.

Twelve weeks after surgery, we reevaluated the patients in both groups. We continued to follow them for 3 years to assess their medical progress and measure depression. At the end of this time, we were successful in locating 34 (32.7%) of the patients, whom we interviewed and tested again.

The results of the presurgical assessment helped the counselors adapt their approach to each patient in the crisis intervention group. Beginning with the first session, the counselors considered each patient's personality and coping style. Some patients took a stoic stance, and counselors listened as they acknowledged, ''If I die, I die.'' Other patients needed reassurance, so counselors listened to their fears and reminded them that, although their fears were understandable, chances for surgery being successful were overwhelmingly in their favor.

Many patients, attempting to protect their loved ones, resisted expressing their emotions. The counselors helped these people by listening to them without passing judgment on what they said. Many other patients denied feeling anxious or worried, and the counselors accepted that denial. In most cases, counselors knew, the denial was valuable protection from unbearable fear. Thus, before surgery, counselors accepted whatever feelings the patients expressed without tampering with their defenses. For patients as well as their families, this approach significantly reduced stress.

During hospital visits after surgery, counselors continued to help patients remember important points about their care, which they tended to forget because of stress. Mitchell McCabe, for example, had not slept for the first 2 days after leaving the intensive care unit (ICU) because he worried his heart would stop and no one would know he was dead. Mr. McCabe was too anxious to remember he was wearing a heart monitor, so he sat in bed afraid to take his finger off his pulse. When the counselor reminded him of the monitor and explained how it worked, he fell asleep before she finished talking.

Sally Kolitz, one of two counselors who guided the patients and their families through the experience, explained, "My most important role was helping patients anticipate what they would experience physically and emotionally. They appreciated the opportunity to explore their feelings, release them, and understand them. These men also valued hearing that their feelings were normal, that they would end, and that the emotions they were experiencing could legitimately follow physiological and emotional stress."

The majority of patients were stoic, controlled men who had never before confronted their emotions, let alone candidly discussed them with someone else. Yet, in the wake of surgery, some became hyperemotional. In outbursts of rage, they could hurl trays of food on the floor. Some became sentimental and could cry at a television comedy. Understandably, the men and their families were confused and frightened by this uncharacteristic behavior. They made good use of the help the counselors offered. "Here comes the lady who lets me cry," became a joke among them.

Nathan Orenstein dramatizes how effectively the counselor's visits eased his emotional pain. From the day this patient left the ICU, he threw every meal tray on the floor. When the nurse brought him a newspaper or magazine, he flung that down as well.

Observing his rage, Ms. Kolitz asked, "What's bothering you? What isn't going well?"

Mr. Orenstein listed a host of complaints: the low-salt diet, noise in the halls, inconsiderate nurses, hurried physicians. The counselor commiserated with his plight. Then, suspecting his anger could be an expression of fear, she commented, "In talking to other patients, I find many say that it's scary after surgery. Do you ever have any of these feelings? Do you ever worry what's going to become of you?"

He peremptorily dismissed any such concern. ''No, no, I'm going to be just fine.''

The counselor dropped the issue for the moment but continued to mention other patients' fears on subsequent visits. Ultimately, this patient let go. Mr. Orenstein was a prominent attorney deeply committed to his work, and he secretly anguished that his career was over. The more Mr. Orenstein talked about his fear, the more information the counselor, nurses, and physicians were able to provide. As he received reliable information, his fears diminished.

Had a well-trained counselor not quieted this man's fears, his anger might not have abated. The experience of a patient who did not receive crisis intervention illustrates this point. When Joseph Cobb seemed unreasonably angry, the nurses tried cajoling him. When that approach didn't work, they tried reprimanding him. Being treated like a child only fueled his anger. It never occurred to the nurses that Mr. Cobb was struggling with nagging fears. As his anger intensified, so did the nurses', until they resorted to avoiding him as much as possible. When discharged, Mr. Cobb was still hostile and argumentative, and his wife worried that he had suffered a permanent personality change.

The psychological tests that the patients took before surgery gave us valuable insight into their personalities. By highlighting strengths and vulnerabilities, the profile enabled the physicians, nurses, and counselors to plan the most effective management of each patient. Phillip Raymond's story illustrates this well.

At 48, Mr. Raymond was a brilliant financial analyst who had experienced chest pain on and off for 9 years. He was competitive and hard driving. In addition, he believed he was invincible, and despite recommendations to the contrary, he smoked, ate the wrong foods, remained overweight and sedentary, and avoided his doctor. Ultimately, his chest pain got worse, and he found himself a candidate for by-pass surgery.

As one might expect, Mr. Raymond always denied his emotions and kept tight control over all facets of his life. He suffered headaches and stomach pains when he became tense, yet he never acknowledged his concerns even to himself lest he appear weak. Mr. Raymond never complained, not when he worried about his health and not when he felt sick. He was a perfectionist, sometimes placing impossibly high demands on himself. He met the ensuing frustration with explosions of temper. During these moments, he felt the hammer in his head, the vise grip on his chest, and the knots in his stomach.

To help Mr. Raymond recuperate with minimal frustration, the medical team capitalized on his need for control. In the hospital, he became unusually alert to sensations in his body. His physician responded to his observations by explaining them at length. Although Mr. Raymond's hypersensitivity to what he was feeling could have bred apprehension, the medical team circumvented that possibility by giving him the opportunity to understand his medical condition fully and participate in planning his rehabilitation.

After surgery, Mr. Raymond healed quickly. Although many patients relinquish some of their denial after surgery, he did not. He insisted he was fine and began doing some work from his hospital bed to prove it. But he became irritable. When the counselor observed that his angry outbursts stemmed from his need to take control over his life, the staff went out of their way to let him make choices and decisions rather than antagonizing or patronizing him. Yet two problems persisted: his immersion in his work and his hostile interactions with his wife and teenage son. To address these problems, the counselor taught Mr. Raymond some relaxation exercises and discussed his need to reassess his professional responsibilities. When she talked to the couple, she invited them to express their respective fears concerning his surgery and other worries the experience had brought to light.

Patients like Phillip Raymond often resort to their old habits as soon as they recover completely. In fact, they quickly convince themselves that they do not have coronary artery disease and that whatever problem prompted the surgery no longer exists. Knowing this, the counselor took advantage of Mr. Raymond's need to control his life and secured his cooperation in designing some new exercise, relaxation, and eating habits. Predictably, he was resistant at first, but he gradually became aware of worries which he had suppressed. He acknowledged them and began to change. Two years after his surgery, he was still working hard, but he admitted he had always been his own worst enemy and lessened his demands on himself. At the same time, he seemed to grow more tolerant of his family.

Conclusions of the Study

We found that 20% of all patients were depressed the day before their operations and all patients experienced intermittent depression during the days and weeks following surgery. But 3 months after surgery, depression fell to 14% among the counseling group while it rose to 24% among those who received standard care. At the end of 3 years, an additional 4% of patients in the second group became depressed, while the number of depressed in the counseling group dropped to just 6%. More significantly, twice as many depressed patients experienced serious medical complications at both measuring points.

While all patients in the Miami study experienced some depression, it was far less debilitating to those who had received counseling. Crisis intervention, it seems, gave this group enough understanding about themselves and their surgery to identify depression, accept it, and do something constructive about it.

In contrast, those without counseling found depression more enigmatic and troubling. In a significant number, the condition was masked. Instead of appearing despondent, these patients complained of low energy, trouble sleeping, poor appetite, and various other ailments. The patients, often in concert with their physicians, presumed these complaints were symptoms of medical problems or failed surgery. But since the symptoms emanated from depression, neither physical examination nor laboratory tests could verify the suspicion.

Interestingly, findings of the Medical Outcome Study, published in the *Journal of the American Medical Association* in December 1989, paralleled our own. This multi-million-dollar project, which tracked the care of over 22,000 adults by 523 health care providers, including internists, cardiologists, psychiatrists, psychologists, and other specialists, found that depression disguised as medical ailments eluded diagnosis in 46 to 51% of cases, depending on the setting in which the care was rendered. While the primary purpose of this study was to compare the quality of care given in various settings, the results show that even in the best situations, up to half of all depression cases do not get properly diagnosed. In our study, debilitating depression occurred most frequently among patients who had experienced numerous or significant life changes during the preceding 6 months and whose surgery entailed many bypasses. Our study suggests that if you fall into one of these categories or if you have periodically experienced depression, you would be wise to arrange for crisis intervention. Otherwise, you probably do not need it.

Even if you are not especially vulnerable, you will probably profit from preparing yourself for surgery in the same way that crisis therapists prepare their patients, and the forthcoming chapters will help. In anticipation of hospitalization, you and your family should know exactly what procedures, physical discomforts, and emotional reactions the experience will entail. You would probably benefit from knowing how others responded at each step, from knowing yourself, and from understanding how you cope best. Inherent in this self-awareness is your understanding of how much control of your life you prefer to take and your ability to adapt this preference to the demands of being a hospital patient.

If you fit the profile of patients prone to postsurgical depression, we urge you to arrange for crisis intervention. Since counseling may keep you away from your cardiologist's office in the future, it is economically prudent as well as practical. We also urge you to select a counselor who is appropriately trained and intuitive enough to be able to provide the special brand of help effective during crisis. He or she should have a master's or doctoral degree in counseling or psychotherapy, know the literature on heart surgery, and have experience working with medical patients. At the very least the professional must be willing to become familiar with the available literature. Your surgeon or cardiologist may be able to recommend a therapist. You can also turn to the psychology or psychiatry department of a local university hospital, the Mental Health Association, the American Heart Association, or a local support group for heart surgery patients.

Crisis intervention is intended to be provided during crisis, not weeks or months afterward, when reactions can become deeply imbedded. We recommend that you begin as soon as you agree to surgery. Ideally, the therapist would meet with you alone, with your family alone, and with all of you together during several short sessions. In this way, you can all get to know the counselor and grow comfortable talking openly. During hospitalization, you would probably benefit from several short visits with the counselor. After discharge, we recommend weekly sessions in your home and with your family. By the end of about 2 months, you will probably feel the crisis has been resolved and be ready for the meetings to end.

Should you not elect to undertake this kind of therapy from the outset but discover the need for professional help later, do not feel that you have made an irretrievable mistake. While it is preferable to prevent the onset of serious depression, counseling initiated at a later date can help.

Whether or not you need crisis intervention, you would probably benefit from an empathetic, loving support system to help you garner your most successful coping strategies. Supporters can provide invaluable help by understanding the feelings you are likely to experience at the various stages of recovery. If your supporters can accept your emotions without feeling threatened, they can help you vent your feelings and restore your perspective.

Gerald Caplan notes that people who successfully weather a crisis emerge more self-confident and better able to cope with future traumas. In other words, difficult experiences hold the potential for growth. If you can utilize the principles of crisis intervention—with or without professional help—you stand to gain more from your surgery than just a healthy heart.

Points to Remember

Heart surgery can be a major life crisis and leaves one-third of patients suffering from debilitating depression. This depression appears to be aggravated by the inability to cope.

❑ Arrange for crisis intervention to help you cope if you have experienced numerous or significant life changes in the last six months, if your surgery entails many bypasses, or if you are prone to depression.

❑ Learn what to expect from every facet of recovery.

❑ Understand yourself, how much control over your life you prefer to have, and how you best handle difficult situations.

Chapter Two

CHOOSING SURGERY

Quite appropriately, the heart is called the pump of life. With its complex structure of chambers, valves, and electrical impulses, this strong muscular organ takes oxygen-rich blood from the lungs, propels it throughout the body, receives waste-laden blood on its way back from distant cells, and returns it to the lungs for cleansing. This is how the system works:

The Pump and Its Operation

Clean blood abounding with oxygen leaves the lungs and fills the left atrium of the heart, which is a holding chamber. A periodic electrical impulse makes the atrial walls contract, and the resulting pressure forces open the mitral valve, one of four one-way trapdoors that keep the blood moving in a single direction. Flowing through the mitral valve, the blood fills the large and powerful left ventricle, the main chamber of the heart. As a charge of electricity emanating from the atrium makes the walls of the ventricle contract, the blood surges through the aortic valve into the aorta, the largest artery of the body and the trunk of the arterial tree. Like an actual tree trunk, which gives way to limbs and smaller branches, the central artery branches off to smaller arteries and capillaries, carrying sustenance to every cell in the body.

After exchanging oxygen and nourishment for carbon dioxide and other wastes, the blood returns to the heart, specifically to the right atrium. When this holding chamber fills, its walls, stimulated by an electrical charge, contract. The resulting pressure opens the tricuspid valve and the blood is released into the right ventricle. When this ventricle squeezes, the blood is propelled through the pulmonary valve to the lung, where it is cleansed and reoxygenated. Then the process is repeated.

The heart can function properly provided that several conditions exist: The walls of the chambers must be intact, the valves must open and close efficiently, the electrical impulses must keep the muscle contracting regularly, and the muscle must squeeze effectively. When people are otherwise healthy and the heart works efficiently, a sense of strength and vigor prevails. But any of a number of disruptions to the complex workings of this organ can cause problems; among them is coronary artery disease, obstruction of the blood vessels that feed the muscle itself. This is the condition that bypass surgery treats.

Circulation to the Heart and Bypass Surgery

The heart, like every other organ in the body, needs blood for sustenance. Ironically, although its chambers are filled with blood, the tissues of the muscle itself absorb virtually none of it. Instead the organ is fed by a system of vessels, called the coronary arteries, which emanate from the first branch of the arterial tree.

When the coronary arteries are healthy, blood flows through them easily. During exercise or stress, when the heart pumps more quickly and needs additional nourishment, healthy arteries can transport sufficient blood. However, as a result of numerous factors working silently for years—smoking, a high-fat diet, excessive stress, inadequate exercise, and genetic predisposition, to name some of them—the coronary arteries can become clogged, preventing adequate circulation. This diminished blood flow usually causes a squeezing sensation or a feeling of heaviness in the chest. It can also cause pain in the left arm and/or the jaw. Often, this sensation, called *angina,* lasts only moments. It may come with physical activity and stop when the exertion stops, signaling that, for an inactive state, circulation is adequate. Although angina may be fleeting, it is warning that the heart is being pushed beyond its limits. If part of the heart muscle is starved for too long, the deprived portion can die and be replaced by scar tissue. This is a heart attack, also called a *coronary* or *myocardial infarction.* It can be fatal if muscle damage is extensive.

Sometimes narrowed arteries inhibit the flow of blood to the heart without the telltale symptoms of angina. When this restriction persists, a heart attack can occur painlessly. These so called "silent" heart attacks are especially dangerous because patients, unaware of the crisis, do not get immediate medical attention. Conversely, severe angina or even a heart attack is not necessarily a threat to life. The location and degree of blockage may be more pertinent than pain or minor muscle damage.

During bypass surgery, blood vessels taken from elsewhere in the body are used to create detours around obstructions in the coronary arteries. The procedure, which provides a pathway for the blood to flow freely, is usually performed to reduce or eliminate chest pain, prevent a heart attack, and improve the quality of life. Under some circumstances, blockages pose an imminent threat to life and must be dealt with surgically. But in approximately two-thirds of cases, there are preferable or alternative treatments.

Other Kinds of Heart Surgery

Bypass surgery comprises about 70% of all heart operations. Of the remaining 30%, nearly all are performed to replace valves—usually the aortic and mitral valves, occasionally the tricuspid valve, but rarely the pulmonary valve—which have stiffened and narrowed or which have started to leak. As the valves work with decreasing efficiency, the heart pumps less and less productively. When one or more valves are seriously impaired, the heart cannot pump efficiently no matter how strong the muscle or how sound its circulation. At worst, faulty valves are life-threatening.

Leaking Aortic Valve

The heart's most important valve—so designated because of its location at the juncture of the left ventricle and the body's main artery—is composed of three pockets that collapse and open as electrical impulses rhythmically cause the heart to contract and relax. When the muscle contracts, blood pumped from the ventricle makes the pockets collapse, permitting flow into the aorta. Like all vessels, this artery is elastic, and it expands in response to the pressure of blood being pumped. When the heart relaxes and the force subsides, the aorta contracts, allowing the blood to backslide. When the valve is working properly, its three pockets open up, catch the blood, and hold it until the next squeeze can force it forward. If the aortic valve leaks, however, the blood can slip back into the ventricle from which it was just pumped.

A leaky aortic valve is most often caused by a childhood episode of rheumatic fever. During adulthood, subacute bacterial endocarditis, an infection of the membrane that lines the heart, can also destroy valve tissue. This variant of the problem causes similar inefficiency. As a result, diminished circulation to the brain makes patients black out or feel light-headed. If insufficient blood reaches the heart, patients can experience angina even though their coronary arteries are healthy. In addition, because the heart muscle must compensate for the leaking valve, it may work so hard that ultimately it fails to pump. As a result, blood backs up and the lungs fill with fluid.

Narrowed Aortic Valve

The pockets of a healthy aortic valve collapse in response to the squeeze of the ventricle and create an opening about the diameter of a quarter. Because of damage from the toxins of rheumatic fever, congenital deformities of the valve, and advancing age, however, the valve can become laden with calcium, which causes it to stiffen. This *stenosis* restricts the pathway through the valve to perhaps the diameter of a pencil point. Consequently, although the blood is pumped vigorously, it can barely squeeze into the aorta. The effect on the heart can be compared to what happens to a garden hose when its nozzle is turned down. Just as water pressure builds up against the hose, stenosis of the aortic valve imposes enormous back pressure on the ventricle and strains the heart. When this pressure exceeds the heart's capacity to combat it, the blood backs up through the mitral valve and into the lung, bringing on heart failure. At the same time, since blood cannot pass easily into the aorta, blood flow throughout the body is compromised. During exercise, patients may suddenly collapse because insufficient blood is reaching the brain. Often, patients just feel faint. If the compromised blood flow impedes circulation to the heart, patients can experience chest pain. Ultimately, a condition called *congestive heart failure* occurs. As the heart loses pumping power, fluid builds up in the body, particularly in the legs, abdomen and lungs. When fluid collects in the lungs, shortness of breath can become a serious problem.

Leaking Mitral Valve

The mitral valve, which separates the upper and lower left chambers and is considered the second most important valve, must be large enough for a full supply of oxygenated blood to pass efficiently from the atrium into the ventricle and strong enough to withstand the enormous pressure generated by the pumping of the left ventricle. This valve, so named because of its resemblance to a bishop's headpiece, or miter, is composed of two adjacent parachutes held to a supporting ring by strong shrouds. As the aortic valve closes during the relaxation phase of the heartbeat, the pressure of blood in the atrium opens the mitral valve, and the ventricle fills up. Then, as the ventricle squeezes, the parachutes open to ensure that the blood continues on its one-way journey through the aortic valve into the aorta. If the mitral valve leaks, the blood is thrust back into the atrium at enormous pressure. Since there is no valve separating the atrium from the vessel that connects to the lung, the blood is forced into the lung, straining that organ and possibly rupturing its vessels. As the lungs fills, patients can cough up blood and experience shortness of breath.

Narrowed Mitral Valve

When the mitral valve calcifies, it inhibits blood flow from the left atrium into the ventricle below, so this important chamber never fills up completely. The heart intensifies its pumping effort to compensate, but less than a full quotient of blood enters the aorta. The resulting diminished circulation makes patients feel dizzy, collapse, and/or suffer chest pain.

Leaking Tricuspid Valve

The tricuspid valve rarely develops problems on its own. It can, however, begin to leak as a secondary consequence to a backup of blood caused by a faulty aortic or mitral valve.

Tumors of the Heart

Aside from valve surgery, a small proportion of heart surgery is performed to remove tumors. In almost all instances, these are noncancerous spongy growths called *myxomas,* which resemble closely bound clusters of soft grapes. They are usually found in the left atrium, the chamber that receives oxygen-rich blood from the lungs. As the tumor grows, it can plug up the mitral valve. Since blood is then prevented from passing freely into the left ventricle, the tumor creates the same problems as stenosis of the valve. The heart is forced to intensify its effort, yet blood flow is compromised. As a result, patients can experience chest pain, fainting, and a buildup of fluid in the lungs, extremities, and abdomen. Alternatively, small pieces can break off from the larger tumor, travel with the bloodstream, and find their way to the brain, where they cause ministrokes. Surgery to remove the tumor cures the condition permanently.

Weakened Areas of the Heart Wall

In another small percentage of cases, surgery is performed to remove an *aneurysm,* or bubble in the wall of the heart, which can develop after a heart attack. When a portion of heart muscle is deprived of oxygen and dies, it is replaced by scar tissue. As the heart continues to beat, this area, which is inherently weak, can grow thin and balloon out, forming a pouch that traps the blood. Like a tumor that clogs a valve, an aneurysm prevents the blood from moving efficiently through the system and causes many of the same symptoms. It is repaired by cutting out the bubble and sewing the resulting hole closed.

Congenital Defects

Occasionally, surgery is necessary in adults to repair heart defects that have been present since birth. The most common of these congenital abnormalities is an *atrial–septal defect,* or hole in the wall separating the two upper chambers. If the structural integrity of these spaces is not secure, waste-laden blood in the right atrium, which is headed for the lungs, sloshes back and forth mixing with newly oxygenated blood in the left atrium. As a result, the blood that falls into the left ventricle and gets pumped into the body is not as rich with oxygen as it should be. Although this condition is present at birth, it may not become apparent until adulthood, when the onset of coronary artery disease or another heart problem tips the balance. Shortness of breath and other symptoms of insufficient oxygen supply result. Together, congenital defects, aneurysms, and tumors account for only 2% of all heart surgeries performed on adults.

Diagnostic Procedures

Perhaps you've had worrisome chest pains for some time. Maybe you've even had a heart attack. Alternatively, you may have been experiencing shortness of breath, occasional blackouts, or feelings of lightheadedness. Possibly you thought you were a model of good health, but then you failed a routine stress test. Any of these scenarios could lead you into a web of diagnostic procedures to define your problem and suggest appropriate remedies.

If your physician suspects your symptoms emanate from a condition other than coronary artery disease, you will undoubtedly undergo an echocardiogram. This is ultrasound, much the same as sonar used by ships to measure the depth of the sea and by obstetricians to peer into a pregnant uterus. In cardiography, high-frequency sound waves transmitted into the chest bounce off the heart as a computer translates the echoes into multicolored images broadcast on a television monitor. The technology has grown so sophisticated that it shows the heart beating, reveals tumors and congenital defects, depicts the valves opening and closing, and permits precise appraisal of their damage. Echocardiography is the definitive test for valve disease. It is a painless, noninvasive, risk-free procedure that enables cardiologists to assess the optimal time for surgery.

If your physician suspects that you are suffering from coronary artery disease, you are likely to undergo a thallium stress test, in addition to a resting electrocardiogram (EKG) and a standard stress test. While exercising on a treadmill, you will receive an intravenous injection of radioactive thallium, a harmless contrast medium that highlights on film areas of heart muscle which are being deprived of blood. This deprivation can be caused by one of two problems: either obstructed arteries, which prevent sufficient circulation to meet the increased demands of exercise, or a previous heart attack, which has permanently scarred the area. To isolate the correct cause, the scan is repeated after several hours of rest. If the second scan shows the area in question to be amply renourished, it was probably starved temporarily because of compromised circulation. If, on the other hand, the picture hasn't changed, it most likely reflects old damage.

The thallium scan can show areas of the heart muscle receiving inadequate oxygen, and it can reveal the evenness of blood flow through the coronary arteries. It cannot reveal how much blood is flowing through those arteries, nor can it image the arteries themselves.

They only way to see inside the coronary arteries is through *cardiac catheterization* (also called *angiography*). Because this study permits an accurate look at the arteries themselves, it is prescribed when an acute heart attack, intermittent angina, or preliminary studies suggest that repair of the vessels may be in order. Catheterization is prerequisite to heart surgery of any type. Where bypass is concerned, it reveals detail essential to planning the operation. In anticipation of other procedures, it alerts the surgeon to any portentous blockages that might trigger a heart attack during or soon after surgery. Thus, the study provides important insurance to surgeon and patient alike.

Coping with Catheterization

Catheterization sometimes requires brief hospitalization, although increasingly it is being done on an outpatient basis. Regardless, most patients are sedated before they are taken into the catheterization laboratory and usually arrive in the lab feeling relaxed, yet alert enough to banter with the professional team and follow instructions to move, breathe

As the contrast material flows through the heart, it draws a map of the coronary artery system and shows the location and extent of any blockages.

deeply, and cough. The procedure, which is performed by an invasive cardiologist (i.e., one who specializes in such procedures as angiography and angioplasty), begins with an injection of a local anesthetic into the groin area of the thigh, which has been shaved and scrubbed as it would be for surgery. For most patients, this injection is the most uncomfortable part of the procedure, but it is no more painful than any other injection. Once the area is numb, the cardiologist, guided by an X-ray image of the heart broadcast on a television monitor, inserts a catheter into the femoral artery and threads it to the heart. Since blood vessels are devoid of nerve endings, this part of the procedure is usually sensation free.

Once the catheter is positioned properly in the coronary arteries, the cardiologist injects a contrast medium through the catheter. Usually, as the dye enters the coronary arteries, patients feel suddenly hot. Some patients, prepared for the heat wave, are surprised when they feel virtually nothing. Others agree it was as unpleasant as they were warned it would be. Occasionally, the hot flush is accompanied by an unpleasant fishy taste, an urgent sense of nausea, and vomiting. All these reactions disappear in less than a minute.

As the contrast material flows through the heart, it draws a map of the coronary artery system and shows the location and extent of any blockages. It also helps to highlight the mechanical functioning of the heart so that the cardiologist can assess the damage to the muscle as well as the organ's efficiency as a pump. To view the entire heart, the cardiologist repositions the catheter inside the main chamber several times and injects more contrast material each time. With every dose of dye, the heat resurges then subsides. The entire study is over in under an hour. Finally, the cardiologist withdraws the catheter—another sensation-free experience—and firm pressure is placed on the artery to prevent bleeding. Although patients must lie still for several hours until the blood has safely clotted, they experience no pain during this time.

When catheterization was initiated in the late 1950s, it seemed an awesome diagnostic tool even to the professionals who used it. Since then, however, experts have refined the techniques, and the procedure has lost its portentous character as well as most of its attendant risks. Nevertheless, patients often approach catheterization with trepidation. It is a natural tendency to fear the results, as though the diagnosis would not exist if the catheterization didn't confirm it. For those who have never experienced catheterization before, it also carries the fear of the unknown. Some patients feel invaded and vulnerable. As one woman put it, "The cardiologist literally touched my heart, and there on a television screen, for all the world to see, was my soul." Occasionally, patients even feel threatened by the consent form.

The consent form for cardiac catheterization—like consent for surgery—ensures that you understand the benefits and risks associated with the forthcoming procedure. It also enables the hospital to prove legally that you were appropriately informed. Ideally, your attending physician will discuss with you at length why this procedure is advisable. In candidly disclosing its risks, he or she will tell you that heart attacks, strokes, kidney failure, and a host of other ominous consequences happen on rare occasion, but that in 999 out of 1,000 cases, the procedure is accomplished without any complication whatsoever. Whether you have this discussion with your doctor or a nurse, by the time it is over, you should feel confident that you are having the study because its potential benefits outweigh its risks.

Still, signing the consent form, which lists in painful detail every remote complication, can be frightening. With luck, you will encounter a good nurse, who will help you understand how safe the procedure is. Our nurses mitigated many patients' fears when they emphasized that signing the consent is a formality and that any patient recommended for catheterization was unlikely to encounter a problem. By the same token, a perceptive nurse can quiet patients' apprehension as they wait for the procedure to begin. One man about to undergo catheterization lay in the waiting area worrying about the anesthetic injection he would get in his groin. A nurse asked him why he was worried and when he told her, she responded empathetically, "We see lots of folks who are scared of needles." Her acceptance of his feelings together with the sedation helped him to relax, and he managed the procedure without difficulty.

While many patients experience some degree of anxiety before catheterization, some feel none. Some are intrigued by the process and become fascinated watching their hearts on a television screen. And when the procedure is over, nearly everyone is surprised at how easy it really was.

Deciding On Bypass

Your catheterization may reveal that you have a dangerous blockage of your left main artery. This is the artery that feeds the left ventricle, the most important chamber of the heart because it is responsible for pumping oxygen-fresh blood throughout the body. Statistics suggest that, if your left ventricle is deprived of blood, you stand little chance of surviving. Surgery is mandatory and often scheduled within hours.

Statistically speaking, surgery will probably also prolong your life if you have 70% blockage in three arteries and minor damage to your heart muscle or if you fall into several other "high-risk" categories, defined in part by your age and the extent of your heart disease.

For many patients, bypass surgery is not prescribed to lengthen life. Rather, its intent is to reduce or eliminate angina so that your life can be more enjoyable. When quality of life is the goal, surgery is usually optional. Whether it is advisable depends on a number of considerations, perhaps the most important of which is pain. How intense is your angina? How much does it interfere with your activities? How effectively can the problem be solved with more conservative management?

Another important consideration is that bypass surgery does not cure atherosclerotic disease, which is an ongoing process. After surgery the agents that clogged your coronary arteries in the first place will continue to deposit plaque on your native vessels as well as your bypasses. True, a healthy life-style can probably slow the process. But surgery is always viewed as a temporary measure estimated to last 10 years. In some patients, the duration is shockingly less, in others surprisingly more.

Surgery has become increasingly safe and effective in recent years, yet it is not without danger. Occasionally, surgery brings on heart attacks and strokes. Less serious complications delay recuperation for perhaps 5% of patients. And a small number of patients are left with lingering neurological and emotional problems that prevent them from recovering fully. Because surgery always carries some risk, most prudent physicians recommend that, if at all possible, you first try managing your condition with medication. Drug therapies have improved in recent years, and many patients find that new medications and new applications of older drugs can successfully dilate their arteries and thereby eliminate their pain without restricting their life-style. For other patients, drugs do not do the trick.

In recent years another option has been developed: *percutaneous transluminal coronary angioplasty* (PTCA), commonly known as the balloon technique. In its simplest form, a catheter is inserted into the femoral artery and threaded up to the heart, as in cardiac catheterization, and a balloon is passed through a catheter to the blocked artery. When the balloon is inflated, it compresses the plaque against the artery wall, thus widening the passage and restoring normal blood flow. In some circumstances, lasers, miniature drills and scrapers, and other high-tech devices are employed as well. And sometimes a wire mesh support called a *stent* is left in place to ensure that the artery remains open. Successful angioplasty accomplishes the same results as bypass surgery at considerably lower cost: financial, emotional, or physical. Recuperation time is reduced to days.

Angioplasty, which was developed in 1977 by the late Dr. Andreas Gruentzig of Emory University Hospital, has quickly risen from an experiment cautiously performed only on very low-risk patients to a commonplace alternative to surgery. Today it is frequently advocated for patients after heart attacks, with blockages in one or several arteries, with unpredictable angina, or with bypasses that have closed up.

While over 150,000 PTCAs are now performed every year, the procedure is not for everyone. In some instances, calcification of the blockages prevents successful compression. Other times, the blockages are located beyond the catheter's reach. Ten percent of cases fail; some of these require emergency surgery, which always carries increased risk. Of the 90% that succeed initially, up to 4% shut down almost immediately. In one-third of cases, obstructions form again in a year or less. Repeat angioplasties have been successful for many patients in these latter two situations. Other times bypass surgery has been an appropriate and effective next step.

In expert hands, fewer than 1 in 1,000 patients die from PTCA. Although the remote possibility of heart attack, other complications, or need for emergency surgery does exist, most experts would agree that, for good angioplasty candidates, the procedure is unequivocally preferable to surgery.

Recently yet another alternative to bypass has emerged: *minimally invasive direct coronary bypass surgery.* This so-called "Band-Aid bypass" utilizes miniature video cameras and surgical instruments to fashion bypass grafts onto the beating heart through a few tiny incisions, some no more than one inch in length. While this procedure holds the promise of minimizing postoperative trauma, it has yet to be proven reliable. To date relatively few of these procedures have been performed, and research suggests that inexperience on the surgeon's part invites complications. On more than one occasion, profuse bleeding or insufficient blood flow—two possible consequences of imprecise sutur-ing—have resulted in the need for emergency conventional bypass. Moreover, Band-Aid bypass is usually recom-mended for people with only one blocked artery, most of whom are candidates for angioplasty. Someday, perhaps, Band-Aid bypass will make conventional surgery obsolete. Today, however, there are few circumstances in which it would be the treatment of choice.

Angioplasty, then, remains the only viable alternative to conventional bypass for most people. When angioplasty is not an option, bypass may be recommended even if it isn't essential to prolonging life or controlling pain. Some pa-tients, for example, have increasingly frequent angina, which a physician may interpret as a signal of future trouble. On the grounds that an elective procedure is safer than emer-gency surgery, the physician may recommend bypass before it becomes mandatory. In optional cases, numerous factors affect a physician's thinking. Patients under 70, for exam-ple, statistically do better than older patients, but many older people do exceedingly well. Even certain high-risk patients can benefit significantly from surgery. In some, it can im-prove the pumping power of the left ventricle. Conse-quently, oxygen-rich blood is delivered more efficiently throughout the body, and the patient gains increased energy and stamina. Yet prognosis can also be affected by diabetes, previous heart attacks, degree of damage to the heart mus-cle, location of the damage, and efficiency of the heart's pumping capability. Chronic lung disease (bronchitis and emphysema, for example), overall health, and gender also color the picture.

A number of studies recently have suggested that bypass is being prescribed excessively in the United States. The conclusion arises primarily from the discovery that, in the majority of cases, patients who were treated medically lived as long as those who had surgery. While these studies cer-tainly underscore the need for prudence in sending patients to the operating room, for several reasons they are limited in their validity. Survival rates were assessed despite the fact that, in most instances, the primary purpose of surgery is to enhance quality of life. Second, the studies looked chiefly at a small subset of the surgical population, and it would be remiss to apply the observations to everyone. Third, in order to evaluate long-term results, they reviewed operations performed more than a decade ago; since then, surgical techniques as well as alternative treatments have improved significantly. If anything, this research further compounds an already complicated issue. With so many factors to consider, recommendations for surgery are often based as much on judgment as they are on objective findings.

When surgery is optional, some patients study their conditions so thoroughly that they almost take a postgraduate course in coronary heart disease and its treatments! For example, Jacques Monteil, a 55-year-old Swiss accountant with an insatiable desire for knowledge, read all of the literature he could find, sought additional opinions from recommended specialists, and consulted numerous patients who shared their experiences with him. Patients often seek information because doing so increases their sense of control over their fate. This is not to suggest that everyone should pursue an intensive investigation. The amount and type of information that is helpful varies among people, and you would do well to follow your instincts in deciding what to learn. When information begins to increase anxiety, it may be time to stop learning.

If you want to participate actively in the decision, read *Bypass* by Jonathan Halperin and Richard Levine or *Open Heart Surgery* by Ina Yalof (see ''Some Additional Resources'' at the conclusion of this book). Both of these volumes explore the anatomy, physiology, and management of coronary heart disease. After this reading, perhaps you should sit down with the experts and talk specifically about yourself. While statistics about risks and prognosis offer valuable guidelines, you are not a statistic; you are a person with a unique health history as well as unique physiological and psychological dynamics.

Since recommendations for surgery often rely heavily on a physician's judgment and perception, it's not unlikely for experts to disagree, as journalist Douglass Cater discovered. Mr. Cater, who chronicled his valve replacement surgery in a *New York Times Magazine* article entitled "How to Have Open-Heart Surgery (and Almost Love It)," acknowledged that he encountered his greatest difficulties when he tried to reconcile conflicting opinions among physicians he respected. Yet he found the act of deciding to have surgery invigorating.

When Jacques Monteil investigated the advisability of surgery, he consulted two specialists and asked each these questions:

Why is bypass surgery better for me than medication?

Can my arteries be repaired using a less invasive technique?

Am I a candidate for transluminal (balloon) angioplasty?

Presuming I am not a good candidate for balloon angioplasty, what factors make me a good candidate for bypass surgery?

What factors stand as potential obstacles? How are the risks balanced against the benefits?

If I agree to bypass surgery, what are my chances for success in light of my unique health circumstances?

Exactly what does success mean for me?

Specifically, how will surgery alter the quality of my life?

When surgery is optional, some patients study their conditions so thoroughly that they almost take a postgraduate course in coronary heart disease and its treatments!

How long are the benefits of surgery likely to last?

What is involved in the surgery and recovery?

What problems can the heart–lung machine cause and what is the likelihood that residual difficulties will affect my life-style? (The heart–lung machine takes over respiration and circulation while the coronary arteries are being repaired. Although this machine is an effective substitute for the heart and lungs during surgery, its use has been implicated in postsurgical neurological difficulties. In the vast majority of cases, these problems are minor and transient.)

Would you create the bypasses using the saphenous vein from the leg, the mammary artery from the chest wall, or both? (In general, the saphenous vein is easier to extract but may become clogged with atherosclerotic plaque more quickly than the mammary artery. Other factors relevant to your particular case will undoubtedly contribute to your surgeon's choice in this regard.)

Although Jacques Monteil's angiogram showed several severe blockages, the two specialists he consulted disagreed about whether he should have surgery. Mr. Monteil sought the advice of a third expert, whose opinion both the others respected. This consultant advised surgery, but Mr. Monteil was still not ready to make the commitment. First he wanted to talk to some friends and acquaintances who had undergone the procedure. He wrote in the journal he kept throughout the experience: "[They] told me about the relief that the operation had brought them and the fact that it had changed their lives. Man doesn't like to live with a sword of Damocles over his head, so after a couple of months of hard thinking, I decided to go ahead with the surgery."

Bypass surgery is not for everyone. Personality and way of life affect the decision. Some patients prefer taking medication to confronting the risk of a surgically induced heart

attack or stroke, even though this risk ranges from a low of
½% in younger candidates to only 3% in older candidates.
One patient explained her refusal to have surgery this way:
"You're alive or you're dead, and when it's you, statistics
don't mean one single thing."

Feeling this way made 47-year-old Donald Lawford resist surgery initially. He had first experienced chest pain
while jogging. After appropriate testing, his cardiologist recommended surgery, but Mr. Lawford wanted to try medication first and switched to a doctor who was willing to go
along with him. For a while, medications prescribed by the
new physician controlled his pain, but before long, Mr. Lawford was experiencing angina whenever he walked. When
he was hospitalized to prevent a coronary, he underwent
another stress test, which confirmed his illness. At that
point, the new cardiologist ordered a cardiac catheterization
and, after reviewing it, recommended surgery.

He said, "We tried medication and it didn't work. Given
your blockages, you will probably have a fatal coronary."

When faced with that alternative, Mr. Lawford agreed
to surgery. He liked the way this physician approached his
illness one step at a time. What Mr. Lawford perceived
as a logical, conservative approach helped him accept the
physician's recommendation for surgery and go into it with
a positive attitude. "If I had been railroaded into surgery,
I would have always wondered if there was some other
alternative that would have been adequate," he said.

Some patients who choose medication initially change
their minds because they cannot tolerate the steady reminders that they are ill. Ivan Kolnikow, for example, tried nitroglycerine for 3 months when he was first given a choice.
Though he was bothered by gripping chest pains from time
to time, his tests showed that his two blockages were not
life-threatening, and he was in no rush to have surgery.

"After a while, I couldn't stand this angina. I never
knew when it would get me. It was like a shadow always

over my shoulder. Finally I decided: Either I'll live like a whole person or to hell with it.''

Other patients for whom surgery is optional take this view immediately. They cannot bear to perceive themselves as ill. Risk or no, they choose surgery feeling that they want to live vigorously or die. Even some high-risk patients feel this way. As one patient admitted, ''My cardiologist told me I had a terrible disease and I know I'm going into surgery with no guarantees. But I'm certainly not going to feel good without the operation, so I'll roll the dice.''

For patients who passionately embrace vigorous activities, surgery is worth its physical, emotional, and financial costs. ''It's a second chance, a new life,'' said one former patient. And he should know. After two heart attacks, he could barely walk around the block. Now he runs, pedals his 10-speed bike over hilly terrain, lifts weights, and, at age 72, just got married for the first time. Like this reborn septuagenarian, most bypass patients emerge from surgery liberated from the clenches of angina and free, often for the first time in years, to walk, sail, or ski the Rockies.

Deciding On Valve Surgery

Compared to evaluating the need for bypass, determining if and when to recommend valve surgery is a more straightforward matter. As long as medication can compensate for faulty valves without diminishing quality of life or permanently damaging the heart, surgery is inappropriate. You don't want to go into surgery prematurely because, although success rates for valve replacement run close to 100%, major surgery of any kind always carries some risk. And some patients with valve disease never need surgery. This is especially true in the case of *mitral valve prolapse,* the occurrence of extra heartbeats caused by a stretched mitral valve billowing into the left atrium. This condition rarely requires surgery.

But if you do need surgery and wait too long, the heart can sustain permanent damage. The backup caused by leaking valves can stretch the heart. When valves are too tight, the muscle works harder to compensate, and it can thicken as a result. If the heart stretches or thickens excessively, surgery becomes much riskier. Moreover, once severely damaged, the heart will never work correctly even if the valves are replaced. So it is important not to delay too long. Most cardiologists would agree that when patients experience severe symptoms—including dizziness, fainting, chest pain, or shortness of breath—surgery is in order. Thanks to echocardiography and cardiac catheterization, the deterioration of valves can be monitored closely and the optimal time to operate can be accurately confirmed.

More ambiguous is whether to replace or repair the damaged valves and, if they are to be replaced, whether to select substitutes made of animal tissue or synthetic material.

The replacement of one or more valves during a single operation has been practiced routinely and confidently since the 1960s. Yet using prosthetic valves of any kind poses potential obstacles. The most common of mechanical valves, the tilting disk or double disk varieties, are made from titanium, plastic, and a hard carbon compound called Pyrolite. While these valves do not function exactly as the valves they replace, they do their job effectively and seemingly forever. Since they are so durable, surgeons usually recommend them for patients under 70. However, the synthetic composition of these valves attracts the formation of blood clots, which could break off, travel to the brain, and cause strokes. To prevent this complication, patients with synthetic valves must take blood thinners for the rest of their lives. These can cause bleeding or complicate bleeding problems that arise later.

Tissue valves offer the advantage of not inducing blood clots, so patients with these implants need not take anticoagulants. Neither do they incite rejection; although the valves used most often come from pigs or are fashioned out of cow tissue, they are treated so that they become biologically neutral. Their one drawback is that they deteriorate in 8 to 12 years, sometimes less, and need to be replaced. Consequently, they are usually recommended for elderly people, whose life expectancy is shorter than that of the valve and who are more likely than young people to encounter bleeding problems if they take anticoagulants.

A third option, especially for patients under 50 who need new aortic valves, is now coming over the horizon as well: implants made from human donor valves. Like pig or cow valves, they do not require that patients take anticoagulants, and they are neutralized so that they do not invite rejection. But they wear out in 10 to 15 years. Moreover, they are trickier to implant successfully than the pig, cow, or mechanical alternatives, and, like all other donor organs, they are in short supply.

Since there is one drawback or another to any prosthetic valve, it would seem preferable to repair patients' own valves than replace them. In fact, modern *valvuplasty,* a procedure popularized by Paris cardiac surgeon Alain Carpentier in the mid-1980s, has been successful, most commonly for a carefully selected population with leaking mitral valves. However, in most instances, the technique is considerably trickier than implanting a mechanical or pig prosthesis. Furthermore, it is difficult to know if the repair has been successful until the patient has been taken off the heart–lung machine and the heart is working on its own. Then, if the valve still leaks, the surgeon must put the patient back on the heart–lung machine and try again. All this uncertainty and its attendant trial-and-error make the procedure more hazardous than valve replacement, even when the combined risk of subsequent surgery to replace worn out tissue valves is considered. Perhaps valvuplasty will come to pass the test of time and the statistics will change. Until then, however, anyone who opts for valve repair needs an exquisitely skilled surgeon, preferably one who suspends final judgment about whether to repair or replace the valve in question until surgery is under way and he can get a close-up view of exactly what he is dealing with.

When you discuss potential valve surgery with your physicians, here are some questions you will probably want answered with the specifics of your own case in mind:

Why are you recommending surgery at this time? What are the disadvantages of waiting? Is there any benefit to delaying surgery?

Which procedure do you recommend for me and why?

What kind of prosthetic valve would you choose and why?

If a tissue valve is recommended: Am I a candidate for a human donor valve? If not, how soon should I expect to have my porcine valve replaced?

If a mechanical valve is recommended: What are the implications of taking anticoagulants? How will they affect my life-style? In what way might they threaten my health in the future?

When valve surgery is performed on the right patient at the right time, it holds all the magic of a miracle. Like bypass, it can turn cardiac cripples into healthy, energetic men and women.

Choosing a Surgeon

It is important for all patients wheeled into the operating room to believe that surgery is the best treatment for their disease and that they are in the very best professional hands. Many people have no trouble acquiring trust and taking their internist's or cadiologist's recommendation for a surgeon. As one patient put it, ''My gut feeling was this guy was good, and that was enough for me.'' He did not feel comfortable interrogating a prospective physician. If anything, the idea of planning the investigation and sorting out conflicting recommendations made him dizzy.

Other people feel uncomfortable putting themselves in the hands of a professional until they satisfy themselves that they have made the best possible choice. Thus, another patient checked his surgeon's credentials in the library, visited his surgeon's hospital, and talked to patients as well as staff. He looked into the ratio of nurses to patients, the role of aides, and the staff's reputation for delivering sensitive, caring attention. Only after this tenacious research did he feel he was making a decision he could trust.

No matter how dedicated to research you are, it is exceedingly difficult to choose a surgeon independently unless you have a sophisticated medical background. If you have the option to choose and feel compelled to participate in the decision, select someone who, at the very least, is a board-certified thoracic surgeon. Certification verifies the surgeon's training and knowledge. You can check physicians' credentials in *Marquis' Directory of Medical Specialists* or the American Board of Medical Specialties' (ABMS) *Compendium of Certified Medical Specialists*. Both of these multivolume directories, available at many public libraries, list more than 300,000 board-certified specialists according to specialty and location. Both include the physicians' ages, where they trained, what certifications they hold, when they were certified, and what hospitals they use. The Marquis publication also summarizes the physicians' careers and thus sheds additional light on their experience.

Where physicians trained and the experts they trained under are important. Look for prominent hospitals with highly reputed heart surgery departments and renowned senior surgeons. In addition, select a surgeon whose performance record compares favorably with national statistics. Nationwide, fewer than 3 patients in 100 suffer serious complication or death from bypass surgery. Can the surgeon you are considering claim the same? If the answer is yes, particularly if this surgeon operates on high-risk patients, he or she is probably a good choice. Before making a commitment, however, you would be wise to ask these questions:

How many procedures do you perform in a day? In a week? (It's important for surgeons to operate swiftly but accurately, especially when patients are on the heart–lung machine. The less time patients are on this machine, the better. When patients are on the machine for longer than 2 hours, the risk of postoperative problems rises significantly. To operate efficiently, surgeons must stay well practiced. They must do enough procedures in a week to keep their skills honed but not so many in one day that they become fatigued.)

How many procedures in a week does your team perform together? With you? With other surgeons? (For surgery to progress efficiently, the team must work in perfect synchrony. When a team works together often, its members mesh with one another like a set of well-matched gears, and they speed the surgery along.)

Since it is so difficult for a novice to select a surgeon, referrals from knowledgeable people can be invaluable. Your cardiologist is probably the best person to advise you. If you ask several physicians and the same recommendation comes up repeatedly, it's probably a good one. Some people say knowledgeable, forthright nurses are the best source for professional recommendations, and usually referrals from professionals are more reliable than recommendations from laypeople. In any case, it is important to evaluate the source of the recommendation and treat the advice accordingly.

Some patients are content when they feel that they have chosen the best trained, most highly regarded surgeon available. They never stop to consider the surgeon's personality.

One patient, who values his vitality more than his life, insisted it would never occur to him to investigate a surgeon's bedside manner: "I don't care if he's the meanest, most insensitive son of a so-and-so who ever furrowed a mother's brow. Just make sure he's a genius with a knife, and let his wife worry about his personality."

For other patients, however, a surgeon's bedside manner is very important. In fact, one of the most frequent complaints of heart surgery patients is that their surgeons neglected them during the postoperative period. Some patients complained they never saw their surgeons after they woke up from anesthesia. More frequently, patients were frustrated because they felt their surgeons' visits, though regular, were perfunctory. While these patients hoped their surgeons would sit down, listen to their hearts, and spend a few unhurried minutes talking and answering questions, the surgeons poked their heads in the door, said something like, "Just checked your chart. Glad to see everything is going well," and disappeared before the patients could formulate a question.

Undoubtedly there are many reasons for this problem. To be sure, heart surgeons are busy and rarely have time for chatting. Patients recovering from surgery, on the other hand, have more time and are more preoccupied with themselves than usual. The brevity of the surgeons' visits may seem exaggerated by contrast. To exacerbate this problem, many surgeons consider heart surgery commonplace. Happily, most procedures are uneventful, and after performing thousands of such operations and watching patients follow a predictable course of recovery, surgeons sometimes forget how important this event is to each patient. Unforgivable though that callousness might seem, in a perverse way it is reassuring.

In addition, many surgeons are better at operating than at communicating and chose their specialty in part because they are more at ease when their patients are anesthetized.

Even those who enjoy spending time talking with their patients sometimes avoid it lest they get too involved. As Tufts University Professor of Psychiatry Richard Blacher, M.D., explained, "The pressures of taking scalpel to body and exploring and even seeming to mutilate the very person he is trying to help may make [the surgeon] hesitate to know the patient too intimately."

Regardless of the reason, the problem is a reality, and if you feel lengthy daily visits with your surgeon are imperative, you should try to assess your surgeon's pattern in this regard. At the same time, since some of the best surgeons are not personable, you may need to compensate. Your cardiologist, your surgeon's physician assistant, a clinical nurse specialist, psychological counselor, or patient educator will visit regularly, answer questions competently and patiently, and thereby assuage your concerns.

With all this attention given to choosing your surgeon, it behooves us to acknowledge that, in the ever-widening sphere of managed care, choices are becoming increasingly limited. More than one person has been faced with the dilemma of being enrolled in a managed care program and finding that the surgeon he wanted—or the hospital or clinical cardiologist of choice—is not on the list of approved physicians. Unfortunately for patients, some of the best surgeons have refused to participate in managed care. If you find yourself in this dilemma, you have two choices: Either you can select a surgeon from the approved list or you can go outside of network. Some managed care plans permit you to choose out-of-network care if you are willing to pay an increased copayment. When managed care does not offer this option, some people have opted to choose the very best surgeon they could find and pay for their operations out of pocket. Should you make this choice, we advise you to talk to your surgeon about the possibility of reduced fees. Many are willing to help you work out a flat fee covering all expenses of the surgeon, anesthesiologist, and other professionals as well as the hospital stay. This arrangement represents an enormous savings over the open-ended fee-for-service charges you would otherwise be billed.

Choosing a Hospital

While many experts contend that the choice of surgeon is more important than the choice of hospital, others believe just the opposite. Regardless of which you select first, hospital and surgeon go hand in hand to some extent because every surgeon admits patients only to certain hospitals. Often, selecting your hospital is another area where you can exercise some control.

Is the hospital you are considering staffed by nurses and technicians who have been specially trained to meet the needs of heart surgery patients? Is the hospital equipped with state-of-the-art technology that can dramatically improve the safety of surgery and the ease of recovery? Here are some examples:

A *pulse oximeter,* used while patients are anesthetized, warns when patients' oxygen levels fall dangerously low before the deficit can cause irreversible damage.

A *carbon-dioxide capnograph* also provides critical information for the anesthesiologist. By graphically representing the carbon dioxide being exhaled, this device reveals how anesthesia is affecting the patient's metabolism. It thus aids the anesthesiologist in the same way that flight instruments guide pilots through storms.

These and other sophisticated monitors and machinery can make the difference between successful and unsuccessful surgery.

Beyond these primary criteria, there are other important factors to consider: Would you prefer a city hospital, where experience is broad but care may be impersonal, or a private hospital, where the opposite may be true? A teaching hospital, where the staff is likely to be aware of the latest research and newest technology, where a house staff—for better or for worse—is on call 24 hours a day, 7 days a week, and where each patient is likely to be the subject of study, discussion, and probing designed as much for the students' benefit as the patient's? Or a nonteaching hospital, where physician assistants may be the most highly trained professionals immediately available? There are pros and cons for each, and the records of individual hospitals, together with their respective professionals and facilities, warrant investigation.

It is always a good idea to ask your physicians which hospital they would choose and why if they were the patients. Unquestionably, cardiologists and surgeons know the various hospitals intimately, and if you are persistent, you can usually get even the most reluctant physician to reveal his or her preference.

In addition, hospital procedures and regulations vary, and all other things being equal, you may make your choices based on these details. For example, in some hospitals, families cannot visit patients once they have been sedated for surgery or while they are in the ICU.

Choosing a Cardiologist

Even though you are in the hospital for surgery, most surgeons want you to be seen regularly by a clinical cardiologist. This physician, whose interests are internal medicine and diseases of the heart, serves as quarterback of the medical team. It is the cardiologist's job, for example, to make sure that medications the surgeon prescribes for your heart don't conflict with different medications you are taking for an unrelated condition. The cardiologist maintains an overview of you as a whole patient while the surgeon, anesthesiologist, and other specialists concentrate on specific areas.

With his broad perspective, the cardiologist balances the narrow focus of each specialist; he makes sure that their respective efforts are properly coordinated and double checks for omissions and errors. The cardiologist is also likely to assume the role of your advocate, to pay you a leisurely visit each day, answer questions, and solve problems.

Ideally, you already have a cardiologist with whom you have established rapport. If you don't or if your cardiologist does not have privileges in the hospital where your surgeon operates, you may have to select one. Your internist or surgeon is a good person to make a recommendation. Left on your own, you should choose an internist who is board certified in the subspecialty of cardiology and who has been elected a Fellow of the American College of Cardiology, an honorary organization recognizing outstanding practitioners. This physician should also have experience at a prominent hospital with a well-reputed heart surgery department.

Choosing an Anesthesiologist

Professionals often assert that the anesthesiologist is the most critical person on the surgery team, yet traditionally, this is one area where patients are given no choice. Usually, patients don't even know who their anesthesiologist will be until this mystery person stops by to say hello before surgery. However, if you wish, you can try to learn about your hospital's anesthesiologists and participate in the choice.

When professionals evaluate an anesthesiologist, they consider his or her judgment and track record. With today's anesthetic techniques, patients receive the desired anesthetic effects with a minimum of risk; they can be asleep, feel no pain, and be subjected to less toxicity than former techniques allowed. But the new techniques demand that a number of anesthetic agents be administered meticulously and that patients be monitored scrupulously.

Each patient is put to sleep by several drugs given intravenously. Once the patient is unconscious, the anesthesiologist inserts an endotracheal tube, which provides an unobstructed channel for the passage of gases and which keeps oral and gastric contents from entering the lungs. This tube is inserted into the patient's mouth, down the throat, between the vocal cords, and into the windpipe. At the moment when the endotracheal tube is put in place, patients are vulnerable and the procedure must be completed in less than one minute. To confound this challenge, anatomic idiosyncrasies, which the anesthesiologist cannot discover until the intubation is underway, occasionally make the maneuver particularly difficult.

Maintaining the ideal balance of drugs is also difficult. Consequently, patients are occasionally anesthetized enough to feel no pain but remain conscious enough to faintly hear the surgeon and nurses. In other instances, patients regain consciousness before drugs that immobilize the muscles have worn off. Though not dangerous, these situations can be frightening and illustrate the complexity of the anesthesiologist's tasks.

Since the anesthesiologist's job is so critical, many patients go into surgery with increased confidence when they have had a say in choosing their anesthesiologist. Moreover, while anesthesiologists often cannot avoid scratching the throat, straining the jaw, or chipping a tooth, patients sometimes hope that by participating in the choice, they will find an anesthesiologist who is particularly gentle.

When asked to recommend an anesthesiologist, surgeons commonly reply, "Everyone on our staff is first-rate." This may true, and all anesthesiologists may have a fine record where serious complications are concerned. Nevertheless, as surgeons and operating room nurses often confide, if they were patients, they would be sure to choose a specific one or two anesthesiologists from among that first-rate staff.

In choosing an anesthesiologist, consider the following:

Is he or she board certified?

How often does he work with heart surgery?

How long has he been at your hospital?

How often does he work with your team?

How well is he respected and trusted by other physicians and hospital staff?

Does he take time to explain what he will do?

Has he been found guilty of malpractice?

Does he see his patients after surgery? (This is a clue to how much he cares.)

One patient, about to undergo surgery in a distant city, called a physician friend long distance to discuss his fears about anesthesia. The friend suggested, ''Ask your surgeon who would be his anesthesiologist if he were the patient. When he gives you the party line, press him. Tell him you're sure they are all fine but that he would have a preference anyway. What would his preference be? He'll probably answer you honestly.''

The patient followed his friend's advice. His surgeon responded as the friend had predicted. And the patient went into surgery feeling confident that he had the best possible anesthesiologist.

Banking Your Own Blood

Despite careful scrutiny and reliable tests for AIDS and hepatitis, there is still a remote risk of contracting these diseases through blood transfusions. In an attempt to protect their patients, most hospitals doing heart surgery have taken a number of steps to reduce the need to transfuse patients with the blood of strangers.

If your operation is elective, you can probably bank a pint or two of your own blood, all you are likely to need. To bank 2 pints, begin 3 weeks before surgery. If you give one pint then and another 2 weeks later, your body will have plenty of time to replenish its loss. If you cannot bank your own blood, family members whose type matches yours can donate blood and have it designated for your use.

Once 75% of patients lost enough blood to require transfusions during and immediately after surgery. However, with the advent of cell-saver technology, blood lost during surgery and the early postoperative hours can be recaptured, processed, filtered, and returned to the patient. This technology reduces the number of patients needing transfusions by about 40%.

Points to Remember

❏ Go into surgery understanding how you will benefit from it and believing you are in good hands.

❏ Ask questions and seek enough information to feel confident of a good surgical outcome.

❏ As soon as you agree to surgery, inquire about banking your own blood or having your family bank blood for you.

Chapter Three

GETTING READY FOR SURGERY

Few people relish being a hospital patient. Some, particularly those who associate self-esteem and dignity with self-reliance, often have difficulty accepting this passive role, and they equate its every facet to repugnant feelings of dependency. These men and women manage hospitalization best when they can participate directly in their care and preserve as much control over the experience as possible. In contrast, others find security in relinquishing decisions and choices to others. They feel reassured by the promise that someone else will take care of them. "Just put me to sleep, do what you want, and wake me when it's over," they might well say. Everyone's instinctive desire for control falls somewhere between these two extremes. If you can approach hospitalization in a way that satisfies your need in this regard, you stand a good chance of managing the experience successfully.

Advance Preparations

To exercise control over their emotions and manage difficult moments before and after surgery, some patients perform conscious relaxation exercises and concentrate on mantras of positive thought. These techniques work best after considerable practice, and if you want to try them, we recommend getting an early start. Joseph R. Feist, Ph.D., notes that people respond differently to different kinds of relaxation exercise, and he offers a variety from which to choose:

1. Lying on your back, tense your feet and then relax them. Squeeze and let go; squeeze and let go. Then tense and relax your leg muscles three times. In a similar fashion, tense and relax each muscle group one at a time until

your whole body is consciously relaxed. Then try to sustain a state of utter relaxation.

2. Choose a single word, such as *one*. Concentrate on breathing slowly, regularly, and deeply. Repeat this word every time you exhale. One . . . one . . . one.

3. Breathe slowly and regularly. Imagine you are blowing away anxiety each time you exhale. Out it goes. It rises up, up, up; it dissipates and disappears.

4. Imagine you are in a beautiful, peaceful place. You are drifting in a rowboat on a calm blue lake. You are lying on soft grass beneath the soothing sun of a May afternoon. You are quiet. You are safe.

5. Imagine a series of appealing thoughts: a tropical jungle dense with dewy green; the chirping of birds, high in the pines of northern woodlands; the sweet fragrance of lilacs; the taste of ice cream, smooth and cold.

In addition to these exercises, the how-to's of Zen philosophies, meditation, and self-hypnosis are available in a wide variety of books and tapes. Experiment, and if you find one or several approaches that soothe you, use them to sustain a state of relaxation for 15 or 20 minutes.

Some patients also find that positive assertions ease emotional distress before surgery and afterwards. By repeating each statement over and over while concentrating on breathing slowly and deeply, they find they can reduce anxiety and quiet their apprehensions. Here are some relevant statements for you to try:

I am having surgery because it will give me a better life than I could have had without it.

My physician believes I can recover.

I may feel frightened (or worried or scared) now, but these feelings will go away.

My strength will resume. I will get better.

For those who dread abdicating control even while they are under anesthesia, a growing body of research should provide some comfort. According to this work, pioneered in part by Henry L. Bennett, Ph.D., at the University of California Davis Medical Center, patients under effective and adequate general anesthesia can receive messages, comprehend them, and act upon them. Dr. Bennett demonstrated this phenomenon by telling anesthetized patients that, when he visited them a few days later, they would pull their left ears. Sure enough, during a postoperative interview, the patients tugged at their left ears even though they could not remember having received instructions to do so and reported no memory of their surgery whatsoever.

A number of studies suggest that patients can use this power to their advantage. According to one, published in Britain's prestigious journal *The Lancet,* for example, anesthetized patients undergoing hysterectomy were told that they would be eager to be up and about in order to speed their recovery. These women were out of bed sooner and suffered fewer complications than those who received no positive suggestions during surgery.

No one can say with certainty that appropriate encouragement during surgery will bring benefit or, conversely, that disquieting sounds will impede recovery. Nevertheless some patients have opted to hedge their bets. Some have equipped themselves with high-quality earplugs to screen out operating room noises. Others, in an effort to create a soothing psychological environment, have used Walkman-type recorders with their favorite music.

If you are inclined to control your psychological environment during surgery, Dr. Bennett recommends using both earplugs and a tape player with the volume turned high enough to penetrate the earplugs. He further suggests selecting a tape player with autoreverse capability, equipping it with fresh batteries, and holding the volume dial where you want it with a piece of tape. Since the anesthetized mind seems to be curiously selective in the way it receives information, he also recommends that if you are interested in positive suggestions as well as music on your tapes, you should enlist the assistance of a psychologist familiar with the dynamics of anesthesia.

Patient Education

The hospital staff will help you find a comfortable level of control over the heart surgery experience by preparing you for the events and challenges you will encounter. At some hospitals, patients tour the operating room and surgical intensive care unit. They see patients newly out of surgery with all their tubes still in place. Then they visit someone whose surgery took place the day before to witness the progress that occurs in less than 24 hours. While nothing can be more reassuring than seeing someone one day after surgery sitting up in bed with no visible tubing except an oxygen cannula, some hospitals are reluctant to subject their ICU patients to this indignity. They resort instead to films or descriptions from nurses trained as patient educators.

Good patient education acquaints patients with all the equipment they will see used in their care. It also includes a description of procedures before and during surgery as well as the sensations patients experience afterward. Many hospitals encourage family members to participate in these sessions in an attempt to reduce their anxiety, encourage communication between patient and loved ones, and thereby foster mutual support. Patients often find that attending patient education classes with their families reduces their sense of isolation.

"After the film, my wife and I talked about what we had seen. It felt so good to have something to talk about.

Somehow, the stress each of us was feeling made talking about anything hard. The film broke the ice,'' one patient recalled.

Talking about the class later helped another couple to clarify what each had misunderstood and enabled them to formulate questions to ask the patient educator when she visited them privately.

''When questions are generated this way, people get a good, solid sense of what's going on. It helps them to ask questions they might think are silly, and, believe me, there are no silly questions in this business. It also helps them to verbalize vague concerns,'' the patient educator observed.

While spelling out procedures and sensations is important, the key component of good patient education is teaching several important skills that you will need to perform after surgery to promote recovery. If you practice these exercises until they become routine before surgery, you will perform them more effectively afterward. Consequently, you are likely to recover more quickly and need less pain medication than you otherwise would.

Much of the work you will have to do after surgery is designed to undo the effects of general anesthesia, which congests and shrinks the lungs. To expand them, loosen and release secretions, and thereby prevent pneumonia, you must begin breathing deeply and coughing soon after your operation. Normally, you wouldn't give these activities a second thought. But with a new chest incision, coughing and breathing are painful and make you feel as if your incision will break open. This cannot happen. Nevertheless, you should learn the techniques that will enable you to clear your lungs productively with a minimum of discomfort.

First you will need to support, or ''splint,'' your rib cage to reduce the pain that accompanies the lung exercises. This is done by hugging a stiff pillow. Since ordinary bed pillows are too soft for effective support, some hospitals provide special ones for this purpose. At other hospitals, patients receive specially designed teddy bears. Squarish and firm,

"Even our toughest men patients come to love them, though they're sometimes embarrassed to take them at first."

these foot-tall cuddly creatures afford perfect support for the chest wound. In addition, they wordlessly convey a message of commiseration and emotional support.

"They're a great hit around here," noted Barbara Friedman, clinical nurse specialist in cardiothoracic surgery at North Ridge Medical Center in Fort Lauderdale, Florida. "Even our toughest men patients come to love them, though they're sometimes embarrassed to take them at first. It's not unusual to see these guys lying in bed holding the bear. And everybody takes them home."

To practice the deep-breathing exercise, take a good, stiff pillow or suitable stuffed animal, place it against your chest, and hug it tightly with both arms. With the pillow in place, inhale through your nose and exhale through your mouth twice, watching your abdomen rise and fall each time. Then inhale, hold your breath for two seconds, and cough twice.

Sitting up with a new chest incision will also be easier if you practice the following technique before surgery: To get out of the left side of the bed, roll onto your left side and pivot your legs so they form an L with your body. Placing your top hand on the bed, use that hand to push yourself up. At the same time, drop your legs over the edge of the bed.

Preoperative Procedures

These days, when most patients enter the hospital on the day of surgery, procedures that once took place after admission now take place before. Your doctor will probably schedule you for blood tests, X rays, and other laboratory work a few days before surgery. Once in the hospital, you will shower with an antibacterial cleanser. You will also be shaved from neck to foot and will probably be given an enema. Before going into surgery, you will be asked to divest yourself of jewelry (though some hospitals agree to tape wedding bands in place), glasses, and hairpieces.

Women may be asked to take off their nail polish and makeup so that the physicians can monitor the color of their lips and nail beds. In the operating room, just before administering sleep inducing drugs, the anesthesiologist will ask you to take out any dentures or removable bridges, which will be returned in the ICU. This preparation can feel terribly degrading.

At some point, you will see your surgeon, cardiologist, and various other staff people. If you have arranged for crisis intervention therapy, the counselor will join the parade. You will also meet your anesthesiologist, who will explain his or her tasks, the drugs they involve, and the postoperative sensations they provoke. The anesthesiologist is your advocate during surgery. The one physician in the operating room who is not scrubbed will take care of any special requests you might have, such as adjusting your tape recorder if you choose to use one. Take the opportunity of this visit to express your wishes. During your conversation, remember, too, to tell the anesthesiologist about all crowns, bridges, and other permanent dental restorations as well as any eye problems, past or present. This information is important since the anesthesiologist's tasks involve manipulating your mouth and moving your head.

Like the anesthesiologist, all the other professionals who visit will describe their roles and ask questions pertinent to their duties. Some will perform a physical exam. Patients often find it bothersome to answer the same questions repeatedly and submit to the same poking by various pairs of hands. ''Why can't I go through this just once and let everyone else get the information in conference,'' one might reasonably ask. Here's the answer: Each physician takes his or her own history and performs her own examinations because someone else's written answers prevent her from hearing how the patient answers a specific question, which is often as revealing as the answer itself. Furthermore, each physician considers what the patient says and what the physical examination reveals from a different point of view. In turn, any one verbal response or physical finding may elicit further queries, which may have relevance to one specialty but not to another.

Take advantage of these visits to run through all your questions and discuss all your concerns. Just as every physician asks the same questions during a medical history, some patients like to ask every doctor the same questions, in part for reassurance and in part to enlarge their perspective. Even though each answer to a given question may say essentially the same thing, the nuances and points of emphasis are likely to vary. Since the stress inherent in the preoperative period tends to make concentrating and remembering difficult, it's a good idea to jot down questions as they crop up and to keep track of key points of the answers. Some patients even record these interviews on tape so that they can replay them later and digest them slowly.

Emotions Before Surgery

By the time surgery is imminent, you will probably have confronted the special emotional significance implicit in surgery to the heart. Culturally, the heart is the home of the soul. Though emotions are actually born in the brain, we speak as though love, pain, courage, and hatred emanate from the heart. Jilted lovers suffer from broken hearts. Cold and callous people have hearts of stone. Candor comes forth in heart-to-heart talks. Children "cross their hearts and hope to die" when they seal a promise, and adults vow their sincerity saying, "I mean it with all my heart." In virtually every culture from prehistoric times, the heart has been synonymous with life and feeling.

Actually, the heart is just one of several vital organs. In fact, the heart can often withstand surgery with considerably less risk than, say, the pancreas or the liver. Bypass surgery, for example, usually carries no more than a 3% risk—astonishing news to patients who assume their chances for survival are 50-50. Moreover, with successful transplants and temporary reliance on artificial hearts, there are more treatment options for terminal cardiovascular disease than for diseases of some other vital organs. These truths do not diminish the heart's mystical significance, however. And characteristically, patients erroneously perceive the period during surgery when their hearts lie still as temporary death. Thinking this way, some patients expect to visit their loved ones in heaven. Some go so far as to face a real conflict: Should they come back or not? Some worry that, once they've seen heaven, they won't want to. Others worry they won't be able to. And occasionally patients emerge from surgery with reports of out-of-body experiences.

It is important to emphasize here that, despite some people's mistaken perceptions about temporary death during surgery, patients are very much alive throughout. While the heart is stopped for repair, the heart–lung machine keeps the brain as well as all other parts of the body well supplied with blood, and brain function never ceases. The point is that, because of the heart's awesome significance, people occasionally approach heart surgery with concerns that may seem extreme. Moreover, these concerns are perfectly normal under the circumstances.

Approaching surgery, some patients seem to have their emotions all worked out. Even a patient with a lifelong dread of blood and needles was able to say that he was more afraid not to have bypass and suffer the consequences than face his fears and go forward. Patients like this have apprehension under control, place complete confidence in their physicians, and enter surgery with philosophical resignation: "If I have to have surgery, so be it."

In contrast, other patients are struck with disbelief. "Me? Bypass surgery? Here I am lying in the hospital, and I still can't believe it."

Often, patients feel intense fear. Some, particularly men who were raised believing that fear is a sign of weakness, express their fear as anger in a variety of ways. One patient, whose surgery was postponed twice, became increasingly agitated, as if the very act of waiting eroded his patience. Other patients complain about the medical personnel, the hospital, or the state of the world in general. Patients may blame themselves for needing surgery. Their tempers may explode unreasonably at the people they love; probably, they're angry at heart disease or at their predicament. They may, on some level, feel angry at the medical personnel because they delivered the bad news. If so, they're unlikely to vent their fury at these people whose care they need, and they misdirect it toward those they love most. Because patients trust the love of their family and close friends, they unconsciously make them a target for undeserved anger. "Why are you hovering over me? Why aren't you around when I need you? Why can't you appreciate the way I feel? Why are you patronizing me?" Some patients make their loved ones feel as though they can't do anything right.

Although each patient approaches surgery with a unique emotional portrait, to some extent all patients experience anxiety. Many worry most about relinquishing their self-control, others dread postoperative pain in the chest and leg, and some fear they will die. Some become introspective and pensive; though they may not verbalize their concerns, what they say and do confirms they are confronting their mortality. They make wills if they don't have them, review their lives, evaluate their accomplishments, and think about the people who have played significant roles over the years. Many patients are openly frightened. As one said, "People do die. You've got to be stupid not to wonder whether you'll ever kiss your wife again." Many, however, manage their anxiety privately. Some, mostly men who were trained from childhood to equate courage and self-reliance with stoicism, preserve their dignity by worrying in silence. Afterward they sometimes admit that silence was painful. If they found themselves in the same position again, they would try to be open about their feelings.

"I've never been good at talking about feelings," one man acknowledged. "Men like to talk about things. Feelings don't fit into words and make me feel uncomfortable. But there I was counting down the days till surgery. I'd look at my wife and wonder, will I ever see her again? She'd look at me and sense I'm preoccupied. But I'm not saying anything and she's not saying anything. I think it would have been easier for both of us if I could've said . . . you know . . . I tried to pretend I wasn't scared, but I didn't convince either of us.''

For some patients, a sense of loneliness pervades, especially the night before surgery.

"I'd close my eyes, and I'd see the same vision in my head. It was night and I was alone in my car trapped on a one-way street jammed with traffic. Slowly, slowly I was propelled closer to the black tunnel at the end of the road. I could see it. I didn't want to go into it. But some force stronger than I was kept pushing me forward. Then I'd open my eyes, and even though I was in bed with my wife, I felt so alone and frightened I almost wished morning would come. And yet I was terrified because I knew it would.''

Fear of this kind, painful though it is, can be very helpful. Dr. Irving Janis, author of *Psychological Stress*, found that patients who displayed a moderate amount of anticipatory fear before surgery appeared to have the best outcome. These patients tend to ask questions about their surgery and rehearse the physical and emotional experiences they will encounter. In Dr. Janis's words, this "work of worrying" serves as "emotional inoculation" to prepare patients to cope.

Michael Strickland, a 35-year-old insurance broker, worked at worrying for the 3 weeks between his catheterization and his surgery. During brief bouts with apprehension, his heart pounded and butterflies fluttered in his stomach. Before surgery, the hospital counselor talked with him and listened to his fears. Despite his anxiety beforehand, Mr. Strickland had no trouble after his operation.

Because the heart carries unique mystical significance, heart surgery can prompt a unique sequence of emotions.

Psychiatrist Richard Blacher, in *The Psychological Experience of Surgery,* summarizes a study comparing the anxiety levels of general surgical patients to those of heart surgery patients. Patients in both groups took psychological tests to measure their apprehension before and after their operations, and the general surgery patients, almost universally, registered dramatically high levels of anxiety, which fell sharply during recuperation. For many heart surgery patients, just the reverse was true. Although most of these patients encountered apprehension at some point before their procedures, it miraculously disappeared the day before. Dr. Blacher hypothesizes that because of the awesome nature of heart surgery, most patients instinctively resort to denial to protect them from fear. If this theory is valid, then the apprehension which bypass patients sometimes experience after surgery can be explained as a delayed reaction, similar to the nervousness which someone perilously close to an accident experiences after the danger has passed.

Compared to the anguish felt by Michael Strickland, the relief from anxiety which patients often experience the day before can be wonderful. One patient, whose first heart attack had occurred 10 years earlier and who had then endured a second followed by increasing angina, claimed he felt no apprehension whatever going into the operation.

"I did not let this get to me at all. I didn't want my sons to think I was falling apart. It was important to show strength to my family," he said, adding that he reassured his family as he was wheeled into the operating room. "I was concerned, yes. Scared, no. Surgery had to be done, so I did it."

Another patient denied ever worrying. Although he acknowledged that patients sometimes die and that the operation is serious, he did not review his will or his life insurance policies. He presumed from the outset that he would survive, recover quickly, and return to work.

A third patient acknowledged momentary misgivings, especially after his patient education class. But, he claimed

Most patients instinctively resort to denial to protect them from fear.

these misgivings vanished quickly. He preferred not to see his family immediately before surgery and went single-mindedly forward.

Journalist Douglass Cater tried hard to draw the curtain of denial over his fear the night before surgery, but he was not entirely successful, so he turned instead to dictating a message of farewell into his tape recorder, just in case. Later, he described his feelings during these dark moments: "It's an awkward exercise and by the time I have finished, I find there is a painful lump in my throat. Somewhat akin to Tom Sawyer's participation in his own funeral."

Some patients deal with their anxieties by forcing themselves to ignore information that frightens them. They don't want to know what experiences to expect. They don't want to go to the patient education classes. Douglass Cater purposely avoided reading all about the potential complications because, he realized, ignoring the risks helped him manage his fear.

Mary O'Donnell also turned her back on her concerns. But the feelings she conveyed in doing so were different from Douglass Cater's—ominously different. She entered the hospital without telling her children or her brother and sister. Lying on her side before surgery, she stared vacantly at the blank wall beside her bed. In a shaky voice, she said that she was not afraid of surgery and that she had a positive attitude. Her only concern was that her physician be aware of her previous surgeries so he would handle her scars appropriately. She had refused to see the patient education film or think about the forthcoming events. She sounded terrified when she said, "I'm not ready to leave this world yet," and she drew the covers over her head.

The difference between Douglass Cater and Mary O'Donnell is the difference between healthy coping and unhealthy coping. When people like Mrs. O'Donnell withdraw prior to surgery, they may be signaling feelings of futility. Since the will to survive is essential to recovering well, such feelings can be catastrophic. Sadness, worry, nervousness, fear, and calm resolve are normal presurgical emotions that enable patients to work out their anxieties. When patients appear depressed and withdrawn, however, they may be signaling danger. Patients who are seriously depressed before surgery sometimes harbor death wishes, which they may not realize or want to admit. Nevertheless, they may view surgery as an easy avenue to death and thus be poor surgical candidates.

Andrew Razin, director of the Psychiatric Consultation–Liaison Service at North Central Bronx Hospital, Albert Einstein College of Medicine, warns of the dangers when seriously depressed patients go into surgery:

> There is considerable evidence to suggest that clinically depressed patients fare extremely poorly at cardiac surgery with a grossly excessive rate of mortality and of serious medical complications. Those who survive the postoperative course seem unlikely to benefit much from the surgery. Such patients should, whenever possible, have surgery postponed while treatment for the depression is instituted.

If you feel overwhelmed at the notion of surgery, if you find yourself dwelling on thoughts of death, if you have a history of depression, or if your family notices an abrupt change in your personality, the problem should be brought to your physician's attention.

Not all depression is portentous. In its least serious form, it is transient and lifts easily. Gordon Griffin experienced this kind of depression. He suddenly found himself feeling hopeless when he was told that his surgery had been preempted by an emergency.

> I was terrified of the prospect of surgery. In my experience, hospitals were places where people went to die, and I was mighty uncomfortable with the implications of lying in a hospital bed. I was even more distraught at the notion of being put to sleep. Someone else would have control over whether I lived or died!

But I had to have the surgery, so I psyched myself up for it. I was into the countdown, and the morning of surgery, the phone rings and I hear that my surgery had to be postponed for a day. You'd think I'd feel relieved because I had been granted a temporary stay of execution. Or angry because I had worked so hard to get myself ready and now I had to do it all over again. But I just went into this blue funk, which is not at all my style.

That afternoon, I got a call from the hospital social worker. She said, "Gee, you must really be angry." I said, "Angry? Why should I be angry? These things happen and it's no one's fault." "Well," she said, "if I had spent weeks preparing myself emotionally and then found out I had to do it again, I'd be absolutely furious. No one should have to do that. The prospect of heart surgery is tough enough without an additional emotional burden."

"Yeah, it began to dawn on me. It wasn't fair. I began to feel this fury bubbling in my gut. First it kind of simmered. Then the bubbles boiled bigger, and I exploded. I was angry all day. I yelled at my wife and I yelled at my kids and I called the surgeon and yelled at his nurse. But I didn't feel blue anymore.

Somewhat more intense was the depression Felix Amatta exhibited. When Mr. Amatta went to his patient education class before surgery, the nurse instructor sensed he felt hopeless and suggested a psychiatric consultation. This man was not emotionally prepared for surgery, the psychiatrist agreed, but the psychiatrist felt that with a little more time, he would be able to manage it. The surgeon postponed the procedure, and when Mr. Amatta was in a better frame of mind, rescheduled it. Surgery was uneventful, and Mr. Amatta recovered without serious complication.

George Coffer was also significantly depressed but his surgery could not wait. Mr. Coffer, always tense, sad, and angry, tended to view life pessimistically. Becoming even more negative and distressed in the face of surgery, he appeared a poor surgical risk. However, a counselor who spent time with him before and frequently after his operation, helped avert disaster. Mr. Coffer suffered brief complications immediately after surgery and needed substantial encouragement to overcome his anxieties and become active.

Because the counselor helped him face his fears, he made a complete recovery albeit with checkered progress. Over the ensuing months, Mr. Coffer sought long-term counseling, which helped him cope with the difficulties of returning to work and maintaining his exercise program.

Points to Remember

❏ Experiment with relaxation exercises and positive assertions to help you manage difficult moments.

❏ Take advantage of patient education classes and visits from professionals to ask all your questions.

❏ Have pencil and paper handy, perhaps a tape recorder as well, to keep track of information you receive and questions you wish to ask.

❏ Practice splinting the chest, techniques for getting out of bed, and lung exercises until you can do them without thinking.

❏ If you or your family feels you are severely depressed before surgery, discuss the problem with your doctor.

Chapter Four

SURGERY AND THE ICU

The mind is a wondrous instrument that enables mothers to bear babies without pain-blocking drugs and soldiers to march into combat. The protective mechanism of the mind works effectively in the hours before surgery as well. To give it a boost, you will receive a sedative about an hour before and, incredible though it may seem, you will probably arrive in the operating room feeling relaxed. Although some patients find this time frightening, they are the exception. Some patients are so relaxed that they doze despite the bright lights and bustling activity around them. Others chat with the nurses and technicians as they perform their preoperative tasks. Thanks to the mind's protective mechanism and preoperative sedation, few patients remember these moments regardless of how alert they seem at the time.

Preliminary Procedures in the Operating Room

Some patients would love it if they could be put to sleep before they were wheeled into the operating room so they never had to see it. Because of occasional unexpected delays and the axiom that patients should have as little anesthesia as possible, this is rarely done. You will be anesthetized in the operating theater at some point during the preliminary procedures. Exactly when depends on the practices of each hospital, and these vary somewhat from one to another.

A number of procedures will take place before the actual surgery begins. Although slight variations are possible, these will include the following: Technicians will affix EKG electrodes to your chest to monitor your heart and prepare several channels from which blood can be drawn, medications given, and vital processes monitored. Conventional intravenous lines (IVs) will be placed in each arm to administer extra fluids. A slim plastic catheter will be fed into the main artery in the left wrist, which will first be numbed by local anesthesia. Connected at the other end to a blood pressure monitor, this line will measure pressure in the arteries and provide an avenue from which to draw blood for analysis. Also under local anesthesia, another line will be inserted near the collar bone into the subclavian vein in the neck and threaded through the heart into the artery leading to the lungs. By constantly monitoring the pressure in these arteries, the anesthesiologist will be able to assess precisely how the heart is functioning while the anesthesia is induced as well as during and after the surgery.

Either during or after these preliminaries, the anesthesiologist will slip some anesthesia into your IV, and you will fall into a deep, pain-free, sensation-free sleep. Unlike patients' experiences years ago, when now-antiquated anesthetic drugs were used, patients today are rarely aware that the anesthesia is taking effect. As one patient put it, "I was awake, and then I was awake again."

Once you are asleep, the anesthesiologist will insert one end of the endotracheal tube into your windpipe. The other end will be attached to a respirator, which will keep the lungs ventilated and permit the anesthesiologist to maintain an exact balance of gases during surgery. This endotracheal tube will still be in place when you wake up and will stay there for several hours, possibly overnight, until the anesthetic has worn off sufficiently for you to breathe reliably and consistently on your own. Next, the anesthesiologist may insert a tube through the nose and into the stomach to help prevent nausea after surgery. This too will be in place when you wake up. Meanwhile, you will be cleansed from neck to foot with an orange-brown antiseptic called Betadine and covered with green sterile drapes. Finally, a foley catheter will be inserted through the urethra into the bladder. The urine, which will drain through this catheter for the next couple of days, will be measured to evaluate kidney function and the possible need for additional fluids or medications.

Bypass and Valve Replacement Surgery

Surgery itself begins when the skin is cut, the breastbone is split, and the rib cage is retracted. If the purpose of surgery is bypass, the vessels used to construct the grafts are prepared at this time. Sometimes one or both of the internal mammary (or thoracic) arteries are used. Sometimes one or both of the large superficial veins of the leg, such as the saphenous vein, are used. And sometimes both types of vessels are employed. When the mammary arteries are to be used, the heart surgeon frees them from the chest wall. To minimize the patient's time under anesthesia, another surgeon simultaneously harvests the leg veins if they are to be used as well.

Once these preliminaries are completed, the thoracic surgeon is ready to expose the heart by snipping the protective sac, or pericardium, which surrounds it. Next, he prepares the circulatory system for detour through the heart–lung machine with the following four-step procedure:

First, he creates an opening in the right atrium, the chamber of the heart which receives blood laden with waste products on its return trip from all parts of the body. Second, he makes a similar opening into the ascending aorta, the main artery which carries newly oxygenated blood throughout the body. Third, he injects heparin, a blood thinner, directly into the heart to prevent the blood from clotting while the heart–lung machine is in use. Last, he fits a tube into each of the two openings. When the other ends of these tubes are fitted into the heart–lung machine, the heart and lungs can be effectively detoured. Now, the blood can pass from the right atrium into the heart–lung machine, where waste products are removed and oxygen is replenished. Then the machine can pump the fresh blood back into the ascending aorta and from there throughout the body.

Coronary Artery Bypass Grafts

Once the heart–lung machine takes over circulation, the heart is stopped and the grafts are set in place. The surgeon usually bypasses all significantly blocked vessels unless they are too small or calcified or unless the blocked arteries enter areas of the heart muscle that have been permanently scarred by previous heart attacks; restoring circulation to these areas would be fruitless. On average, three or four arteries are bypassed, although surgeons occasionally do five or more when branches of the main arteries are individually obstructed.

To implant each graft made from the leg vein, the surgeon makes an opening in the aorta (the main artery carrying freshly oxygenated blood out of the heart) and another in the occluded artery beyond the blockage. By sewing one end of the vessel into each opening, the surgeon can reroute the flow of blood around the blockage. With the internal mammary artery, the procedure is slightly different. The surgeon sews the end of the artery that he had freed from the chest wall earlier in the operation into the coronary artery beyond the blockage. With the other end of the artery still attached to its source, this bypass serves as a back door, so to speak, through which blood can flow into the heart beyond the blockage.

Valve Replacement

To replace the aortic valve, the surgeon makes an incision into the aorta above the valve. He then snips away the defective mechanism but leaves the supportive ring, to which the prosthesis is securely fastened. Replacement of the mitral valve is similar. The valve is approached by an incision in the left atrium. The shrouds that hold the valve to its supporting ring are snipped, the failing parachutes are removed, and the prosthesis is sewn to the supporting ring in their place.

Usually just one valve needs to be replaced, but replacing two is not uncommon. Three-valve surgery is rare. Sometimes, bypass is performed at the same time. How much is done to the heart is not, in itself, significant. More important is the amount of time the patient spends on the heart–lung machine. Ordinarily, surgeons do as much as a given case dictates or as much as they can without keeping the patient on the heart–lung machine for too long; after about 2 hours, patients become significantly more vulnerable to complications. During routine bypass operations, patients remain on the heart–lung machine for 45 minutes to an hour. Each valve takes about 45 minutes to replace.

Once the repairs are completed, the surgeon double-checks his work to make sure all seals are perfect and then permits blood back into the heart. As circulation resumes, the heart usually starts beating spontaneously, although it may need an electrical boost. Once it is beating, the anesthesiologist administers protamine to counteract the blood thinner that was infused into the heart to prevent clots while the heart–lung machine was in use. At some point near the end of surgery, two chest tubes are inserted into the chest cavity through an incision beside the rib cage. These permit residual blood and fluids to drain out of the chest after surgery and will remain in place for 2 days. Through all these procedures, the patient's EKG and blood pressure are monitored vigilantly. Only when the surgeon and anesthesiologist are certain that the heart is functioning properly is the heart–lung machine disconnected and the chest closed.

Waking from Anesthesia

Just as people in their own beds sometimes awake confused about what day it is or where they are, so patients often awake from anesthesia feeling bewildered. One patient recalled that as he awoke, he thought surgery hadn't started yet and wondered when it would begin. Then he heard his son shouting, seemingly from a great distance, "Your surgery is over and you're fine."

Another patient remembered total confusion. "I couldn't figure it out. Am I in surgery? Am I dead? Am I in the ICU? Then I heard someone mention Valium. That was a familiar term, so I figured I was alive, but I couldn't open my eyes. I struggled and struggled, but they wouldn't open. Then someone opened my eye and shined a light in it. I had a chance to see for a second, so I was sure I was alive. I had a great sense of relaxation and well-being. I knew I was OK."

Because it is so common to awake from general anesthesia feeling disoriented—after heart surgery or any other surgery—and because residual anesthesia makes people forgetful, the ICU nurses make a point of repeating the critical message. "Your surgery is over and you're fine."

"You're fine." That means that the electrocardiogram, which monitors the pace and rhythm of the heartbeat, shows that your newly repaired heart has tolerated being stopped, cooled, handled, fixed, rewarmed, and restarted. "You're fine" also means that the monitors which register blood pressure in the arteries and veins indicate that your blood is flowing properly and that the incisions are clotting effectively. It means that the blood samples which are periodically drawn and analyzed reveal that respiration is satisfactory. And it means that the urine output shows the kidneys functioning appropriately. Does it mean that you feel good? Probably not.

One patient described her first day after surgery this way. "I didn't have sharp pain. The drugs took care of that, and anyway, I've had abdominal surgery and, for me, the incision in the chest wasn't nearly as painful. I didn't hurt, but my chest felt like I had been hit by a Mack truck. My mouth was dry, and my body was soaked with sweat. I was so hot, and I couldn't move, and I couldn't get comfortable."

"Your surgery is over and you're fine."

Perhaps when you awake, you will be most conscious of the various tubes and catheters that have been plugged into your body: the IV lines, the foley catheter, the catheters in your wrist and neck, the nasogastric tube, two chest tubes, and the endotracheal tube connecting you to the ventilator. Admittedly, the image of a normally independent person immobile in bed serving as a human socket for various tubes is less than appealing. Yet, it didn't hurt when these catheters were affixed. During surgery, these lines permitted exact evaluation of your physiological responses and were therefore invaluable for your protection. And now, they provide the easiest avenue for giving medications and drawing specimens. In the first days after surgery, these tubes will be removed one by one. With the exception of removing the chest tubes, which can be momentarily painful, taking out the lines causes no discomfort. And each time one is removed, you can feel assured that you are making progress.

Managing the Endotracheal Tube

When you regain consciousness, you will become aware of a tube in your throat and the sensation that something is inflating and deflating your chest. This is the respirator, which is breathing for you because the after effects of anesthesia prevent you from breathing on your own. As these residual effects wear off and you can begin to breathe independently, the respirator will provide intermittent support. As soon as you can breathe reliably on your own, the tube will be removed.

Bluntly put, breathing with a respirator is no fun. As patients begin breathing independently, they frequently do not synchronize their breathing with the respirator. Instead of inhaling as the respirator pumps air into the lungs, they try to inhale as the respirator draws air out of the lungs. This tug of war can make them feel that they aren't getting air, and they panic. This is not a serious problem, but it can be frightening. The nurses in the ICU are acutely sensitive to this difficulty, and they are always on hand to coach patients and help them relax. If you encounter this problem, the nurse will probably tell you to stop breathing. If you stop trying to breathe on your own, you will stop fighting the machine and the sense of panic will disappear.

Under normal circumstances, after you stop breathing for a short while, you feel desperate for air. This feeling occurs when the blood needs oxygen. On the respirator, however, oxygen is fed to you continuously, so this feeling does not occur. You can successfully stop breathing, permit the respirator to do its job, and eliminate the sense of panic.

Once you are breathing independently enough so that the respirator provides only intermittent support, you may occasionally hear the respirator beep. This is not the signal of emergency. Rather, it is a reminder to breathe. The machine will guarantee that you get sufficient air. The nurses will be with you and will help you manage the respirator. While this is not a pleasant time, it is a safe time, and the nurses will help you get through it. Implementing relaxation techniques can be very helpful as well. So can repeating mantras of positive thoughts and concentrating on beautiful, sensuous images of another time and place.

Another difficulty with the respirator occurs during the moments when the intubation tube is cleared by suction, yet this procedure is vitally important. Before you can breathe deeply and perform your coughing exercises, suctioning is the only way to remove the secretions that formed in the lungs as a consequence of anesthesia. But the procedure puts pressure on the chest and makes you feel starved for air. Fortunately, the respiratory therapists are aware of the sensation and go out of their way to minimize it.

By the time your endotracheal tube is first suctioned, you may feel comfortably secure with your respirator. Before your therapist can perform this maneuver, the respirator must be turned off. This alone can be alarming. But before you can feel starved for air, the therapist will use a hand respirator to fill your lungs, and he will help you relax before continuing. To remove the mucus, the therapist will insert a slim (one-eighth inch in diameter) catheter through the intubation tube and withdraw the fluid. This is when the sensation of choking occurs. It lasts only a few seconds and is not, in any way, indicative of danger. In between aspirations, the therapist will give you extra oxygen, and at no time will you be deprived of air. The entire procedure, including rests between suctionings, takes less than 3 minutes.

The last problem with the respirator occurs because the tube lies between the vocal cords, and while you are intubated you cannot talk. Again, the ICU nurses, who stay at the bedside almost continuously, are so experienced in the case of patients newly out of heart surgery that they can anticipate many of your thoughts, questions, and wishes. Nevertheless, not being able to communicate can be frustrating. One patient suffered because his lip was pinched between his intubation tube and his teeth, and he couldn't let the nurse know. Another patient awakened from surgery and felt frustrated because he couldn't ask all his questions about the operation. A third patient, so eager to convey his thoughts, tried scratching a message onto his nurse's arm.

Some former patients suggest a pencil and note pad to ease this frustration, but others feel that between the stupor of the drugs and the discomfort of having their arms strapped to IV boards, writing is difficult at best. Another patient recommends working up a list of questions and statements in advance and having a family member bring this into the ICU so you can simply point to your thoughts. You can also facilitate communication by working out your own brand of sign language with your family beforehand.

Ironically, patients occasionally worry about having the intubation tube removed. Some are concerned about discomfort from the procedure. However, with a cough from the patient and a gentle tug from the anesthesiologist or respiratory therapist, the tube usually pops out without pain or other difficulty. Some patients also worry that they won't be able to breathe on their own. This fear, too, is unfounded.

"The last thing we want is to have to reintubate a patient," said Alan Stillerman, a respiratory therapist. "We can tell whether they're breathing efficiently by a simple blood test, and when we take a patient off the respirator, we know that patient is ready." When the endotracheal tube is removed, patients are routinely put on supplemental oxygen to ease their breathing.

The best thing about being intubated is that it is over quickly. In the early years of heart surgery, patients often had to endure this apparatus for several days. Today, however, improvements in anesthesia permit the endotracheal tube to come out as soon as a few hours after surgery, so it is not nearly the misery it once was. In one patient's words, "After that tube came out, I felt confident I would be OK. I was so relieved to have survived to that point, I was just able to relax and let the nurses take care of me."

Other Support Devices

Although patients under general anesthesia are said to be "asleep," the metaphor is erroneous. In terms of the physical and emotional insult the experience imposes, surgery could be compared more accurately to a marathon. The strain can be so severe that it temporarily compromises the heart's ability to function, especially if the muscle has already been injured by several heart attacks. Support devices are employed to compensate. These technological advances keep the heart beating productively while permitting it to recuperate so that it can take over on its own.

Pacemakers

The need for assistance in regulating the heartbeat is so common in the first few days after surgery that patients are routinely equipped to use an external pacemaker. Just before closing the chest, the surgeon attaches a pair of fine wires to the heart. Protruding through the skin, these wires can be connected to the pacemaker if necessary. When this pacemaker is no longer needed, these wires are easily and painlessly removed.

When the electrical system of the heart remains faulty or when the patient must take medications that might slow the heart unduly, a permanent pacemaker must be implanted. This is accomplished in a minor surgical procedure, usually under local anesthesia, in which wires to the heart are attached to a tiny battery-operated computer chip, which is surgically fitted beneath the skin either just below the collar bone or high in the abdomen. Modern pacemakers permit patients to live normally. Batteries last for about 10 years. Though frequent checkups were once needed to ascertain that the device was working correctly, new technology now requires only occasional examinations. Interim inspections, if needed, can be accomplished over the telephone.

Intra-Aortic Balloon Pump

When heart problems temporarily diminish the organ's vigor, an intra-aortic balloon pump can be used for assistance. This pump can also be employed to support the heart before surgery if necessary, and it has proven beneficial to patients waiting for heart transplants.

The balloon, which is inserted via catheter through the femoral artery in the leg, is positioned in the aorta, the main artery coming out of the heart. At the other end, the catheter is connected to a machine outside the body which inflates and deflates the balloon in synchronization with the heart's rhythm. By collapsing at the very instant the heart beats, the balloon allows the heart to pump against minimal resistance. Then, by inflating during the heart's resting phase, it propels the blood forward.

This lifesaving device is used commonly, usually for a day or two, but it can stay in place for a couple of weeks after surgery if necessary. The machine is quiet and the balloon causes no pain, though patients may be aware of a gentle thumping as it inflates. The primary complaint about the device is the limited movement it permits. Because the balloon's catheter is tethered to a machine, patients must remain in bed and fairly still while it is in place. But usually the apparatus is removed before patients feel much like moving.

Beginning the Work of Recovery

In spite of pain medication, it is not uncommon for discomfort to intensify as the lingering effects of anesthesia wear off, and most patients would prefer to be left alone during this early postoperative period. Much as they crave rest, however, they must begin the work of recovery: breathing deeply, turning from side to side, and sitting up. These activities can be quite a chore at first. And while they may be tiring and painful, they cannot, repeat cannot, hurt the heart, dislodge the bypasses, or open the incision.

Martha Weinman Lear, who chronicled her husband's heart disease and surgery in a passionate narrative entitled *Heartsounds,* describes the discomfort her husband experienced as he dutifully tried to follow orders shortly after his bypass operation:

> He had to cough to bring up mucus. That was imperative. If mucus were to block a bronchial tube, lung infections might develop.
>
> But in order to cough, he had to do what was diametrically opposed to instinct, which was to immobilize the chest. . . . One day a nurse suggested that he clutch a pillow tightly against his chest when he coughed, to help hold the chest wall together. [This is splinting, which was described in the preceding chapter.] That helped tremendously. He also discovered that if someone slapped his back, midway between the lungs, he could get up the mucus more easily.

And so we developed a routine: he would sit up, legs hanging over the edge of the bed, pillow clutched in his arms. "Okay, hit me," he would say. "Again—a little higher, a little to the left; there, there, hit," and at the moment I hit he would squeeze the pillow hard and cough and up would come, sometimes, a bit of mucoid matter—such a pathetic return for what it cost him, but a triumph nonetheless, a costly affirmation of life, health, restoration.

Once you are capable of taking deep breaths on your own, you will do your deep breathing exercises with the aid of a contrivance that measures your progress. These "incentive spirometers," as they are called, come in several varieties, and they require the kind of exercise you were taught before surgery: two deep breaths in through the nose and out through the mouth, and a third breath in followed by waiting for 2 seconds and coughing twice. If you cannot expand your lungs sufficiently on your own, you will begin with a device something like a manual respirator. This intermittent positive pressure breathing (IPPB) apparatus forces air into the lungs. Later, you will graduate to an incentive spirometer. Which appliance you start on is unimportant. What is important is that you expand your lungs and loosen the secretions so that pneumonia does not set in.

Also important is the notion that, just hours after your chest has been opened and your heart repaired, you will be capable of performing these exercises, that you can turn from side to side in bed and sit at the edge of the bed, and that in a few short hours you will make your way to a chair.[1] The power of the human body to heal itself is indeed remarkable.

Disorientation in the ICU

Though intubation is uncomfortable and exercising difficult, by far the most troubling aspect of the ICU is the disorientation that occasionally occurs.

[1] If an intra-aortic balloon pump was necessary, this activity will be delayed until the balloon pump is removed.

Actually, it's a wonder that patients encounter as little disorientation as they do. Though modernization is slowly coming to ICUs and some of the problems of ICUs are being solved, in most cases the physical setup itself promotes disorientation. Many intensive care units are windowless wards, always light, always noisy. Ordinarily, these large, open rooms are lined with beds. Men and women lie separated from one another by only a curtain. Beside each bed is a full array of medical equipment—monitors, respirators, oxygen tanks, and IV trees that clank, rattle, beep, whirr, and whoosh. Periodically, a new patient is brought in after surgery, and occasionally a catastrophe occurs. Each of these events spurs additional commotion. In the middle of the arena sits the nurses' station, where telephones ring and where staff members hold conversations with little thought to keeping their voices hushed.

Into this chaos, where day is indistinguishable from night, patients emerge from heart surgery. Pain medication enables them to drift in and out of sleep. However, this medication also makes lights seem brighter and noises louder than they actually are. At the same time, pain medication lowers people's tolerance for light and sound. Though patients are in a state of stress, they cannot release that stress as people commonly do—by moving—and although they crave rest, rest in the ICU is next to impossible. Sleep deprivation aggravates the other problems, and disorientation can result, particularly among older patients. (Older patients may have atherosclerotic plaque in the arteries that lead to the head as well as in their coronary arteries. If plaque restricts the blood supply to the brain, the likelihood of confusion and disorientation increases.) Among all patients, nightmares are common, as are semi-awake hallucinations.

In the ICU, one patient saw huge black creatures whenever he closed his eyes. He recalled, "It was very surreal. I knew I was hallucinating, but that didn't make me feel any less terrified, and I strained to keep my eyes open. I couldn't close my eyes and rest until I was moved to my private room, and then—poof—I wasn't haunted anymore.''

Once patients leave the ICU, these problems almost always vanish. Being in a more restful environment, where night is quiet and days are filled with recognizable structure, helps patients to reorient themselves. As they get out of bed and walk around, the circulation to their brains improves as well, and the monsters disappear.

In the early days of bypass surgery, severe mental disorders were an everyday event in the ICU. As the technology of bypass surgery improved and as patients grew to accept the surgery as commonplace, the frequency of psychological difficulty declined. Today it is rate, probably because most patients are out of the ICU within 24 hours after surgery. Yet temporary emotional upheaval seems more predominant among heart surgery patients than among other patients in the same environment. Tufts University Professor of Psychiatry Richard Blacher observed that among lung surgery, heart attack, and heart surgery patients assigned to the same ICU, severe difficulties were most likely among the heart surgery patients.

In the rare instances when psychosis in the ICU does occur, patients usually perceive their nurses as wanting to hurt them. This paranoia results from convoluted mental processes that work this way: Patients emerge from surgery feeling miserable and vulnerable. ''Just turn out the lights, turn off the noises, and leave me alone,'' they wish. Contrary to these wishes, the nurses are forever turning them, suctioning them, and changing their IVs. Normally, this kind of treatment would enrage someone desperately wanting to be left alone. However, patients know that their lives depend on this care and they fear that if they become angry, the nurses will neglect them. So instead, they twist their anger and see it coming from the nurses instead of from themselves. This unconscious mix-up makes patients perceive their caretakers as hostile. Thus, a physician who became a patient in the very ICU where he had worked for years struck his nurse on the third day after his surgery!

Patients who worry that their nurses are out to hurt them usually realize that their perceptions are distorted, so they keep their thoughts secret. For years, some worry that they were crazy and that they will go crazy again. This fear is unfounded. Paranoia usually disappears permanently as soon as patients leave the ICU.

Despite the miasma of medication, patients are surprisingly alert once the anesthesia wears off, and they are often aware of what is going on around them even when they appear to be dozing. Unfortunately, sometimes they are alert enough to pick up fractions of conversations, but fuzzy enough to misinterpret what they hear or see. Thus, one patient misinterpreted the numbers on his blood pressure monitor and panicked that something dreadful was happening inside him. "It's so important to air your fears," this patient advised. "If something doesn't look right or if you hear something frightening, call the nurse and ask. An explanation can be very reassuring."

Complications in the ICU

Although being in the ICU can be unpleasant, it is unquestionably the best place for patients newly out of surgery, for it is the ideal setup for catching complications. Opening the chest and manipulating the heart is, after all, major surgery. If superficial cuts or everyday hang nails can become infected, it should not be surprising that complications of various kinds can and do occur after surgery. For example, during the first 8 to 12 hours, postoperative bleeding or the formation of blood clots sends perhaps 3 to 5% of patients back to the operating room. Usually this occurs before patients wake up from surgery, so they are rarely aware of the complication until it is history. And, while the incident can frighten the family, surgery is the safest way to solve the problem and rarely prolongs recovery.

Other potential problems include imbalanced electrolytes, wound infections, fevers, and irregular heartbeats. As a consequence of surgery, the electrical system that regulates the heartbeat can be disrupted, causing the heart to beat too slowly, too quickly, or unevenly. These palpitations can be frightening when they suddenly make your EKG monitor beep or create the feeling that horses are galloping in your chest. But palpitations are easily and quickly corrected. In addition, particularly among patients whose hearts were pumping inefficiently before surgery, extra fluids may build up in the lungs and elsewhere in the body.

A patient who had this problem laughed as she told this story:

> The doctor had just finished examining me and turned to the nurse and said, "She's in failure." Oh, my God, I thought, I'm dying. I just lay there and thought about my life and my grandchildren and I wondered if I'd ever see them again. The nurse must have noticed something was wrong, because she asked me. I said, "I heard the doctor say I was in failure." So the nurse said—she was smart—"Mrs. Melatta, do you know what that means? Failure is short for congestive heart failure and it just means that your body is retaining too much fluid. It's probably from the extra fluids you got during surgery. We'll give you a diuretic to take care of it." Sure enough, I was fine, but it's so easy to get scared.

On rare occasions, heart attacks, strokes, perforated ulcers, and kidney failure occur. Patients with diabetes are slightly more vulnerable to kidney failure. Mild heart attacks immediately before, during, or after surgery occur in 2 to 4% of cases and often do not delay recovery. The risk of serious heart attack is less than 1%. Strokes are similarly rare in younger patients, but become a major concern with patients older than 75. In earlier years, when the technology surrounding the surgery and use of the heart–lung machine were relatively primitive, these complications were more prevalent, and, as Martha Weinman Lear's book *Heartsounds* conveys, they are tragic. Today, however, permanent neurological problems are rare. When complications such as strokes or kidney failure involve body systems outside the expertise of the cardiologist or surgeon, these doctors consult with an internist who specializes in the area of the patient's problem. Similarly, cardiologists sometimes consult with their colleagues if a patient has a particularly menacing arrhythmia or other cardiac complication. These consultants, as well as the team approach to patient management, ensure the best and most comprehensive care. If you or a member of your family feels that your complications are excessive or that your progress is unreasonably slow, ask your doctors for a consultation with another expert. Most physicians do not take offense at such requests. In fact, they often welcome the opportunity to confer with a respected colleague. A consultant may shed valuable light on your difficulties. At the very least, another opinion may confirm your physician's views and thereby help to assuage your worries.

Complications, serious or slight, understandably cause anguish and fear. But it helps to remember the statistics: one out of 10 patients encounters some kind of setback. While the likelihood of complication varies with each patient's age and unique medical profile, as many as 99.5% of patients recover without serious setbacks. In part, the risks are so low because they are spotted and treated swiftly. This is the value of the intensive care unit. Here, computers register vital body processes and help keep medications properly controlled. Every emergency and diagnostic tool is immediately available. And specially trained professionals provide expert care and constant attention.

"Thank God for those nurses," said an 85-year-old man who, because of several postoperative setbacks, spent more than a week in the ICU. "My Annie, she was an angel. She knew just how to fix the pillow under my knees. She would wipe my head with a cold cloth. I'm a foolish old man, I guess, but in those gentle hands I felt love."

Older patients tend to recover more slowly than younger patients, and those with damaged heart muscles usually have more difficulty than those whose hearts are healthy, but almost everyone improves. One 65-year-old patient illustrated this miracle of recovery. He had emergency bypass surgery after a serious heart attack. In the ICU he was disoriented for 3 days. His heart rhythm and blood pressure took nearly a week to stabilize, and throughout that time his cardiologist worried that he might die. Although most patients stay in the ICU no more than one day, this patient could not be moved for 8 days. Finally, he was able to leave the ICU, and 2 days after that, he greeted guests in the solarium at the end of the hall.

Ironically, even in the ICU, progress occasionally brings difficulties of its own. As patients become more alert, they are often troubled by the realization that they can't remember the hours immediately before and after surgery. This amnesia is a normal function of the mind's protective mechanism. If you encounter this problem and find it distressing, ask your nurse or your family to help you reconstruct the missing hours. Others are troubled by the realization that they have gained weight, literally overnight. These pounds represent the excessive fluids that were pumped into the body during surgery and will disappear before discharge. And some patients become aware of new and troubling emotions. Sometimes, though they are aware that their surgery was life-saving, they grieve for their bodies, which they perceive as mutilated, and even some strong men may become tearful. Other times, people—particularly those who crave control over their lives—feel frustrated by their helplessness and dependency on machines and medical personnel.

A middle-aged woman experienced this fury shortly before she was moved from the ICU.

I was sitting up in bed breathing this cold dry air [supplemental oxygen] and just feeling furious. My husband asked me why I was so angry, and I told him I felt frustrated because I was powerless. He knows me so well. He patted my hand and gave me a terrific suggestion. ''You're so intent on having control,'' he said,

"Why don't you just decide to exercise your control over yourself?" So I did. I really worked at being cooperative. It was a good plan for me.

Discomfiting though all these problems are, you will not become aware of them until you begin to feel better, so in their own way, they are a sign of progress. Next step: a regular room.

Points to Remember

❑ In anticipation of the time in the ICU when you are intubated, think about how you will communicate and make plans to put your strategy into effect.

❑ You will probably feel calm going into surgery and will not be aware of being put to sleep.

❑ In ICU, do your best to relax and permit the nurses to take care of you.

❑ Try not to fight the respirator.

❑ If you see or hear anything that worries you, ask your nurse about it.

❑ Disorientation, amnesia, and weight gain are normal.

Chapter Five

STEP-DOWN CARE

"Praised be the moment they wheeled me out of that intensive care unit. I just knew the worst was over," one patient exclaimed.

Most people greet this move with joy. A regular hospital room signifies medical progress and promises rest. Yet a regular room can feel disconcertingly strange after the ICU routine. Patients who found the constant attention of medical personnel comforting sometimes worry that, once in a regular room, their problems will go unnoticed. Sometimes just the change in surroundings, personnel, and routines feels threatening.

Under any circumstances, moving from a familiar environment to an unfamiliar one causes stress. When people have been ill, all their vulnerabilities are exaggerated, and their vulnerability to moves from one hospital setting to another is no exception. Patients recovering from heart attacks, for example, sometimes suffer setbacks attributed to stress when they are abruptly transferred from the coronary care unit to a regular hospital room. However, if patients are told about the transfer in advance and if they are moved by people they know, they encounter less difficulty.

These findings translate readily for heart surgery patients leaving the ICU. Ideally, hospital personnel whom you know—a counselor, nurse, patient education specialist, aide, or orderly—will accompany you during the move or visit soon after. Perhaps you can arrange for your spouse or children to be present. At the very least, take the opportunity to ask about your new home. The most important question is this: "How, in this less intensively supervised environment, will anyone know if I am in trouble?"

Telemetry

Any hospital with a good coronary care program reduces the supervision of its bypass patients gradually. Patients leaving the ICU move to a room where each patient's heart continues to be monitored. In many hospitals these rooms form a separate "telemetry" unit. In some hospitals, they are scattered within a general medical–surgical unit. Regardless of the setup, patients continue to have their heart rhythms monitored either by a beside EKG or by a beeper-like device that they wear and that records every heartbeat on a television monitor at the nurses' station. This monitoring is so scrupulous that often, when an irregular heartbeat occurs, doctors and nurses are attending to it before the patient realizes what has happened.

During the first days out of the ICU, nurses are never far away. Patients don't even get out of bed without a nurse standing by. Little by little, the nurses lengthen their tether, and by the time the heart monitor is removed, patients have had ample time to gain confidence in themselves and their newly repaired hearts. From the first hour in the telemetry unit, however, the theme is independence. Hospital personnel think of patients not as sick but as recovering from surgery. This recovery demands that patients assume responsibility for taking care of themselves.

"If patients are going to leave this hospital to lead normal lives, they've got to see themselves as independent," said clinical nurse specialist Barbara Friedman. "We didn't operate on them so someone else could take care of them."

Reestablishing Independence

Predictably, patients respond differently to this firm attitude. Those who relish taking control of their lives often embrace every facet of this responsibility in an attempt to minimize the passivity that hospital routine imposes on them. With the go-ahead from their nurses, they devise a strict schedule for walking, resting, and practicing breathing exercises. They monitor their reactions closely and report any concerns to their caregivers.

Under any circumstances, moving from a familiar environment to an unfamiliar one causes stress.

While all the possibilities may not be immediately apparent, there are, in fact, several ways in which you can take charge. Responsibility begins with accepting the commitment to work in the face of discomfort: try to stand up straight even when your chest incision seems to pull your shoulders down; walk without a limp even if your leg incision begs to be coddled, breathe deeply when it feels as though another cubic centimeter of air simply won't fit.

"I was determined to follow orders to exercise," one patient acknowledged. "I said I was doing it for my family, and I have no doubt that their encouragement was part of my motivation. But secretly, I did it for myself. Setting a goal and striving to meet it—how can I explain it? It was a challenge. It was a triumph. It was like beating my own record in the 50-yard dash."

You can also take charge of your pain medication. Increasingly, hospitals are literally putting pain control into patients' hands with a computerized system called patient-controlled analgesia (PCA). If your level of pain warrants it, you will be able to administer relief as you need it—by pushing a button to release a predetermined dose of analgesic directly into an intravenous line in your arm.

Pain medication works best when the blood level of the drug stays constant. So long as the medication keeps a lid on your discomfort, you need a smaller dose of medication to sustain your relief than you would to overcome intense pain. The beauty of PCA is that it permits you to administer tiny doses of medication at the very instant you feel the need. Doses are calculated individually for each patient, and the computer is programmed to prevent overdosing. Thus, PCA is safe. Moreover, because it permits you to keep a relatively constant blood level, the technology affords nearly optimal relief with a minimum of analgesic. At the same time, PCA enhances your sense of dignity and control.

By the second postoperative day, pain is almost always managed with pills. But whether your medication is administered orally, by injection, or by PCA, you can monitor your pain medication and make sure you receive it frequently enough to keep your pain from building up.

Although your medication is prescribed according to your weight and the time estimated for the drug to take effect, physicians tend to undermedicate. Moreover, when doses are ordered every 4 to 6 hours, nurses often deliver the drugs closer to the 6-hour interval. To compound the problem, many patients try to hold off taking pain medication as long as they possibly can. Some are worried about drug addiction, others contend that taking pain medication is bad, though they cannot articulate why. Still others feel that being stoic is proof of inner fortitude. Regardless of the reason, when patients do not get their analgesics frequently enough, they encounter more pain than necessary and require larger doses of analgesic to get relief.

You have little reason to worry about drug addiction. Numerous studies have documented that patients who take narcotics to control pain have no trouble stopping the drugs when they no longer need them. And don't try to be stoic. You will not be able to rest effectively or exercise vigorously if you are in pain. Consequently, by holding off on your pain medication you can actually impede your recovery.

Do monitor your pain vigilantly. And do make every effort to get your medication frequently enough that your pain is reduced to discomfort.

There is a difference between pain and discomfort. Discomfort implies an unpleasant awareness. It is mild enough that it remains in the background, but it is definitely present. Pain, in contrast, screams for attention. It prevents reading, moving, even listening to conversation. Pain is demoralizing and exhausting. If you are to work at recovering effectively, you need your analgesics frequently enough to prevent your pain from building up. If your analgesics fail to reduce pain to discomfort or if you find huge swings in the degree of pain you feel between doses, you must report the problem to your nurse. She can often juggle the dosage and scheduling of your drugs. These adjustments can make a difference in the relief you get and, in the long run, reduce the quantity of medicine you take. In addition, it's a good idea, if possible, to take pain medication 45 minutes to an hour before doing physical therapy or respiration exercises. This timing ensures that the medication is delivering the maximum relief when you need it most.

It is not uncommon, particularly in hospitals with nursing shortages, for patients to complain that their pain medication is delayed excessively. If you encounter this or a similar problem, take it up with your nurse and, if she cannot help, with the physician in charge. In the unlikely event that the physician fails to respond as well, you can turn to whomever your hospital designates as the patient's advocate. Personnel structures vary among hospitals, but in any good one you should be able to identify someone who will speak on your behalf. Perhaps it is a nurse supervisor, a patient education specialist, a clinical nurse specialist, or a social worker. By the time problems erupt, you and your family will probably be well enough attuned to the hospital hierarchy that you or someone close to you can identify the appropriate resource.

As for other medications, you should know about each drug you take—what it is, what it does, and what its potential dangers are. This is an ideal time to pay attention to that information.

Constipation, an unpleasant side effect of pain medication and the sedentary nature of recovery, is another area where you can take charge.

"Make sure you're getting a stool softener," advises a nurse turned patient. "Drink lots of water, unless you are having problems with water retention. And make a concerted effort to eat vegetables, fruits, salads, and fiber cereals." If the fruit and vegetables that come on your hospital tray look unappetizing, you might consider asking a friend or family member to bring some fresh fruit from home.

While some patients seek every opportunity for responsibility, other patients prefer to relinquish their care to others. Patients who embrace a passive role sometimes find it difficult to overcome inertia. Such was the case with James Nicholson. At 61, he had a 10-year history of chest pain. His father had died of heart disease at age 46, and his brother had had a severe heart attack 3 years earlier. Mr. Nicholson's angina, which grew steadily worse until he had surgery, together with his family history, convinced him that he, too, was doomed. Although surgery quieted his angina, Mr. Nicholson had trouble overcoming his fears. Once out of ICU, he was afraid to challenge himself. He quickly—too quickly—gave in to weakness and fatigue. He complained that even modest physical therapy exercises drained his energy. Worse, he dreaded leaving the hospital and was not eager to hurry his progress along.

Patients like James Nicholson, who have been conditioned to fear exertion by years of pain, often resist testing their surgery, especially if they worry that their discomforts suggest continuing heart disease. If you are disinclined to work at recovery, you must find a way to overcome your resistance. Since the heart is a muscle and muscles thrive on exercise, you must participate in your recovery exercises or you will not benefit from your surgery. If you avoid exercising because you are frightened by sensations in your chest, you must learn more about what you are feeling.

Everyone has pain at the incision site, which is reduced to discomfort by medication. When you first wake up from anesthesia, you will be aware of this pain as well as the pain from your leg incision. By the third or fourth day, your pain should be reduced to a mild annoyance and should be controllable by pills rather than injections. The various healing pains that you experience do not worry your doctor, and they shouldn't worry you.

Some patients say with assurance that healing pains are distinctly different from angina. Angina responds to nitroglycerine; healing pains do not. While angina tends to come with exertion in general, pain from incisions and muscles strained during surgery is more likely to be associated with specific movements, even breathing.

Admittedly, these descriptions are less than definitive. Pain is highly subjective and personal, and when people are concerned about their health, they can become confused about their perceptions. Do not worry in silence. If you are confused about how to interpret your pain, discuss it with your doctor, nurse, or physical therapist. Nurses and physical therapists see hundreds of patients recovering from heart surgery, and they are in a particularly good position to evaluate your pain. Ask them if they think your pain is unusual, and try to describe what you feel. Is the sensation sharp or dull? Does it fell like a squeeze, a stab, a stick, or a weight? Is it intermittent or sustained? What activity or position causes it? Does it occur at a predictable time of day or night? What other sensations come at the same time? What relieves the pain? The more specifically you can describe your pain, the more accurately the professionals can diagnose its cause. If you are convinced that your pain is not dangerous, you will have an easier time persevering, and persevere you must.

Getting well is a lot of work.

The Nature of Recovery

Even patients who embrace the work of recovery, however, feel tentative and uncertain. "Was my surgery a success?" nearly everyone wonders. "Will I be able to walk to the bathroom? Play golf? Return to work? Make love?" These concerns are natural, particularly since recovery is not characterized by steady improvement. All patients have good days, when a sense of progress and well-being prevail, and bad days when everything seems to be a problem. Aches and pains, fatigue, weakness, and other minor setbacks happen routinely, and when they occur, worry and frustration often follow.

"I think we tend to jump to conclusions too quickly," a patient observed. "The minute I felt good, I expected I'd always feel good. Then, when I felt less good, I was sure something terrible had happened."

Most patients are unusually alert to their bodies now. They measure every inch of newfound strength and worry that every twinge might signal a setback. Another patient observed that insecurity breeds apprehension. A physician himself, he recalled being obsessed about a sensation in his chest that he couldn't identify. "During surgery, the sac of tissue that surrounds and anchors the heart had been cut. So my heart felt more mobile in my chest than usual. Lying on my left side at night, it felt as though my lung was being compressed with each heartbeat. I worried about that until I realized what it was."

Anger

Harbored fears erode the temperament, and when patients are worried, whether consciously or unconsciously, they sometimes become uncharacteristically irritable. Paul Stevens, for example, became argumentative and stubborn shortly after he was moved out of the ICU. Always reasonable and cooperative before, he now refused to take his medicine or even look at his tray at mealtime.

Months after his surgery this patient revealed:

There was one nurse who dropped by every afternoon just to talk. She could sense when patients were upset. She'd come in and sit down on the edge of the bed as though there weren't anything else to do in the world. She asked about my wife, and I told her the whole story. It was a second marriage for both of us. We were married just a year when I had my surgery. Laura was working and visiting me and trying to do everything around the house. And of course, she was worried. As I told this nurse all about my wife, I began to realize that I was scared for Laura, and scared for myself, and scared for us. Talking to her helped me to gain a new perspective on my anger.

Anger is a common emotion in the days and weeks after surgery. To observers it often seems unwarranted, and it is often misdirected at the people the patients love most. Sometimes, it is disguised fear, but not always. It can stem from the frustration that patients experience when they tackle the tasks of recovery diligently and feel their bodies aren't responding quickly enough. And sometimes it grows out of a sense of impotence, which comes from lying in a hospital bed.

The best antidote to all these emotions is talk. When people address their problems, they take the first important step to resolving them. Fortunately, under the stresses of this hospital experience, emotional controls loosen, and many people can reach a level of candor they never had before.

For example, Diane Murray was able to address the denial she clung to before her surgery and resolve her anxieties. "I couldn't admit that I was worried before the surgery," she acknowledged some weeks after her discharge from the hospital. "It was as though if I admitted I was scared, something terrible would happen, and as long as I kept a stiff upper lip, everything would be fine. Afterward, though, the reality hit. Now, I can accept that I have heart disease. I can accept my mortality. And I can concentrate on exercising, eating right, and prolonging my life."

For Tony Mendoza, the biggest problem was feeling like a child.

"It's bad enough you have to exercise when they tell you and take your medicine when they tell you. But you can't even eat when you want to. They bring you this trash somebody calls food, and expect you to eat it whether you're hungry or not," he complained to the nursing supervisor.

"You'd rather have some nice lasagna at a candlelit table for two?" she suggested.

The next evening, Tony Mendoza sat down to dinner at 7, the time he usually ate dinner at home. With the nursing supervisor's encouragement and assistance, Elizabeth Mendoza made her husband's favorite dish, which she reheated in the microwave oven in the nurses' lounge. It wasn't quite the same as dinner at home, but it helped to reassure Mr. Mendoza that he was a man who had the power to make a decision.

Despite the frustrations, the recuperative powers of the body carry on. Just a few days after surgery, most patients—even men and women well on in years—look healthy. They can cough, breathe deeply, and do their physical therapy exercises without apparent distress. Wearing bathrobes and slippers, these patients stand casually in the hall chatting with each other and their visitors. They are amazed at the speed of their own progress.

Yet this well-being is a fragile thing, as one patient's experience dramatizes:

"I was feeling great," 50-year-old Marvin Dolan recalled. "I really was doing very well. I had had a lot of company. We talked and joked, and when they left, I walked them down the hall. I didn't realize it at the time, but I had overdone it. The next day, I had no steam at all. It took a few days before I regained the ground I had lost."

Marvin Dolan's tenuous perch between growing strength and impending setback is typical. As patients inch forward, they often become unusually contemplative. It's common for bypass patients to reevaluate their philosophies and priorities. Many ponder the possibilities of changing to less stressful jobs, retiring early, spending more time with their families. Even hard-nosed business people frequently turn nostalgic and sentimental. As Wall Street lawyer Steven Danforth coined metaphors about red and yellow leaves dancing outside his window, he sounded more like a poet than a hard-driving senior partner.

Steven Danforth, never sentimental, was suddenly wistful about autumn landscapes. Diane Murray, who had never acknowledged feeling anything but fine, was admitting she had been too afraid to face her fears. Mild-mannered Paul Stevens turned ugly and irascible in the days after his surgery. People who have always prided themselves on their stoicism dissolve into tears without apparent provocation, and understandably, they worry they have permanently lost their self-control. Such changes in temperament, especially when they are characterized by up-welling emotions, occur frequently as patients settle into the second stage of recovery. These changes are temporary and usually vanish within a couple of months.

Depression

On the fourth or fifth day (perhaps sooner and perhaps not until weeks later), many patients encounter depression, sometimes for the first time in their lives. For some, the depression amounts to no more than fleeting blue moments. Others experience a dense fog of hopelessness and despair.

"It's a rare patient who experiences no reactive depression whatsoever," said counselor Sally Kolitz. "But these feelings are normal and self-limiting. Painful and frightening though they may be, they are not serious."

Amy Foster recalled the moment depression hit her, on the fourth day after her surgery. "I was standing over the sink in the bathroom washing my hair, and I started to cry. I didn't feel particularly sad or worried, but I couldn't help myself. I just sobbed my heart out. Oh, what was happening to me?"

Diane Murray said her depression set in when she suddenly became convinced she would never recover. "I was so elated when they told me I could leave the ICU. After I was in my room for about an hour, the nurse came in to help me get into a chair and moving was tougher than in the ICU. My chest incision hurt more, and I felt so weak I thought I would sink right through the chair. I was devastated."

"You bet I feel blue," said Michael Conran, a 35-year-old insurance agent who had emergency surgery while he was on a business trip 2,000 miles from home. "I've just got a new job, and I'm wondering if I'm gonna keep it. I live to play baseball, and I'm not sure I'm ever gonna swing a bat again. Not this season, that's for sure. I've just spent 6 months building up my body in the gym, and now I'm gonna lie here and watch it go soft.''

Another patient echoed this young man's concerns when, on his third postoperative day, he worried if he would ever ski again or whether he would always feel deprived because he couldn't eat his favorite chocolate cake.

Patients whose very survival lifted them into euphoria sometimes claim they never felt true depression. The subdued feelings they called depression were nothing more than subsiding ecstasy. For others, feelings of hopelessness weigh heavily. Regardless of degree, these emotions and the tears that frequently accompany them are a natural response to an overload of emotional and physical stresses. After all, every patient who reaches this point has, within the recent past, confronted his mortality, surrendered to the manipulation of his body, trusted his very breath to people he barely knows, and returned to consciousness in the cacophony of the ICU.

All patients are weakened by the operation and the anemia that normally follows it. Many become exhausted in the ICU, where they find sleeping difficult. To make matters worse, they receive pain medication that triggers depression as a side effect. Is it any wonder that the mind rebels? Controls are loosened as the mind takes time out to heal itself. Anger, poor concentration, memory loss, difficulty reading and thinking of words, and seemingly unprovoked weepiness occur when the mind steps off guard. Blue feelings and tears can descend spontaneously on and off for up to 3 months, and then gradually, they recede. And then, for most patients, they disappear.

To ease depression, be realistic in your expectations. Since heart surgery causes major physical and emotional disruption, healing takes a long time. Gains are tangible, but they are sometimes small, sometimes halting. Even after patients are home, the gains play tug-of-war with weakness and fatigue. When fatigue sets in, everything hurts more and emotions are more difficult to manage. Gradually the good days win out. But although the majority of patients can resume most of their activities within a few weeks, many admit it takes months, some say a year, before they feel like themselves in all respects.

Consequently, you will do yourself a favor if you expect the pace of recovery to be slow and uneven. Conversely, if you are impatient with yourself and unrealistic in your short-term goals, you will set the stage for depression.

In addition to having realistic expectations, you can benefit from accepting depression and other unusual or uncharacteristic emotional reactions with equanimity. If you understand that these emotional shifts are normal and temporary, you will work through them more quickly than if you harbor fears that surgery mutilated your mind.

During this period, patients occasionally report disturbing memories of their surgery. It is possible, we now realize, for chance remarks made in the operating room to filter through the anesthesia and take hold in the subconscious, often in grossly distorted ways. If you feel burdened by any such memories, fear not that you have gone crazy. But do share your recollections with your surgeon, anesthesiologist, or someone else present in the operating room. You will probably find it reassuring to have your memory put into its proper perspective.

Since emotional controls are loosened after heart surgery, patients who had unusually frightening experiences years before occasionally dredge them up. One patient, for example, relived his childhood horrors as a prisoner in Auschwitz. Although he had successfully coped with these memories for more than 50 years, during the week after surgery he began to be plagued with nightmares so terrifying that he contemplated suicide. Occurrences like this are rare, and usually temporary. They are best managed by talking them through, preferably in consultation with a professional counselor.

Although emotional distress is troublesome, you and your loved ones should not find it threatening, provided you see two things: one, that it lifts from time to time; and two, that it is not so oppressive that it keeps you from the activities that promote recovery. If depression becomes deeply entrenched, you may stop caring about whether you develop pneumonia or circulatory problems. If you stop caring, you may stop doing your deep breathing and physical therapy exercises, and you will fail to progress.

With the physical aspects of recovery, as with depression, patients' experiences vary. Many have no difficulty coughing or breathing deeply after the third or fourth day. Yet others complain that the respiratory therapy is the most agonizing part. Some patients complain about their incisions when they walk and about a general numbness in their chests. Other patients are bothered most by shoulder and back muscle strain, a result of the rib cage being retracted during surgery. Still other patients say they never feel unbearable pain but find they are periodically overcome by weakness and exhaustion. Others worry about their inability to concentrate and gaps in their memory—both normal byproducts of heart surgery and its attendant anesthesia, medication, and stress.

During this phase of recovery, do not be surprised if you feel nauseated and find food distasteful. Anesthesia, medications, and electrolyte disturbances can all contribute to this problem. Eating well promotes healing, however, and on the basis of this rationale you may indulge in your most tempting favorites, even a corned beef sandwich or chile con carne.

Clinical nurse specialist Barbara Friedman advises, "During recovery, the body needs a full range of nutrients to repair itself. At this point, it's much more important for patients to eat well than follow a diet plan. If they would enjoy a rare steak and french fried potatoes, bring them in. When patients eat the foods they enjoy, they get a psychological lift, too. When their appetite returns in a week or two, that's the time to get serious about lowering fats and cholesterol."

Winking, she added, "It makes the families feel awfully good when they can bring in food. It's great when they can make a positive contribution to the recovery of the person they love."

Medical Complications

No matter how dedicated patients are to promoting their recovery, complications occasionally thwart the progress. As a rule, older and sicker patients encounter more difficulties than younger, more vigorous patients. Older patients are especially vulnerable to strokes, which can be fatal. Patients with atherosclerosis of the arteries that feed the head may suffer from tiny clots in their brains. These can cause neurological symptoms and can affect word recall and memory sometimes for months.

Smokers, like people with asthma, chronic bronchitis, and other lung diseases, are bound to have more trouble than nonsmokers. During the early postoperative hours, when patients are intubated, smokers need to be suctioned more frequently than nonsmokers. They find the breathing and coughing exercises more painful, and they recover more slowly.

As one patient who had been on oxygen for 8 days after his surgery put it, "I smoked for years. Now I'm paying for it."

Whether patients smoke or not, they occasionally confront wound infections, systemic infections, clots in the lungs, and an inflammation in the chest called postcardiotomy syndrome, which causes fever, other flulike symptoms, and depression. Some 40 to 50% of patients experience abnormal heartbeats. Although these arrhythmias can be severe, they are usually not serious. Understandably, however, they can be distressing, especially when they occur after patients have been taken off their telemetry monitors and then have to be reattached.

One cardiologist and former patient explained:

> In this business, every step is a mark of progress or regression. In the ICU, every time they take out a line, you think, aha, I'm moving along. Then you leave the ICU—more progress. Then you can get out of bed unsupervised. Then they take you off the monitor, and you figure you're almost home. Then you fibrillate [experience irregular or extra heartbeats] and you're back on the monitor. I'm a physician. I should know better. But when it happened to me, I really got bummed out. I was convinced I'd never get better.

He did, of course. Almost all patients do. One of our patients, 69 years old, suffered from such severe angina that he could barely walk before his surgery. When he entered the hospital, his blood pressure was so low he was nearly dead. He was in the ICU 8 days and had a dreadful time with postoperative psychosis. After 17 days in the hospital, he went home and was fine.

Another patient, 60 years old, should have had an easy time because, except for his clogged arteries, he was healthy and vigorous. But 8 days into recovery, he developed a wound infection and clots in his lungs. Although he stayed in the hospital nearly 3 weeks, he left expecting an uncompromised recovery.

Almost always, complications are more distressing than they are serious. And almost always they can be corrected.

Resolving Concerns

Throughout the recovery process, but especially when unexpected concerns arise, patients and their families yearn for explanations and reassurance from their surgeons. Sometimes, surgeons offer veritable panaceas in their daily visits. They listen to their patients' hearts and comment on what they hear. They sit down, answer all these patients' questions, and ask questions of their own, indicating that they are aware of and concerned about each patient's unique circumstances. All too often, however, the surgeons remain maddeningly out of reach. At worst, they don't visit and they don't return phone calls. More commonly, they are present, but distant and aloof. Even when they visit daily, they frequently hang onto the door post as if to say, "Don't expect a lengthy conference." When patients yearn to tackle their list of questions and sense their physician's impatience, their frustration and fear can intensify.

You need not endure this frustration passively. Certainly the surgeon is an ideal person to answer questions. If you wish to speak specifically to your surgeon, make this request, and set an appointment for a time that is convenient for him. Sometimes, physicians remain distant for fear that, given the chance, their patients will trap them in endless conversation. To counter that worry, you might approach your physician saying, "I have five questions I'd like to ask you," or "I need 15 minutes to talk to you. Could you please arrange that for tomorrow?"

It's natural to feel that since the surgeon fixed the heart, he's the best person to answer questions about it. But this presumption isn't necessarily so, especially for surgeons who are better at operating than communicating. On the other hand, many nurses are knowledgeable professionals trained to educate patients. A patient educator or clinical nurse specialist can probably provide thorough, satisfying answers. So can your cardiologist, other physicians, physician's assistants, and the therapists who work regularly with heart patients.

Occasionally, patients openly express their fury at the unavailability of their physicians. Confrontation can be unpleasant, but patients who draw battle lines because their physicians won't satisfy their need to talk are conquering the bigger struggle. They are feeling well enough that they can concentrate on something other than their own survival. How refreshing to be able to solve problems like these!

During this second stage of recovery, we found that patients' concerns tend to follow a predictable course. At first, they worry about setbacks, later about dependency. And as the period of hospitalization after heart surgery has shrunk in recent years, patients sometimes worry about being discharged from the hospital before they are ready. While it is true that the push to reduce hospitalization has come from the need to contain hospital costs, especially on the part of managed care organizations, it is equally true that improvements in medical care have hastened the pace of recovery. When recovery follows a routine course and the heart is functioning properly, patients are ready to leave the hospital after 4 or 5 days, sometimes after just 3. If your recovery progresses more slowly, however, or if you are beset by complications, any decent physician will keep you in the hospital as long as necessary. Whenever you are discharged, you can feel confident that it is safe to continue your convalescence at home.

Points to Remember

- ❏ Do your lung and physical exercises religiously, if possible, about an hour after taking pain medication.

- ❏ Request your analgesics before your pain has the chance to build up.

- ❏ Talk to your nurse and doctor if your pain is not kept at a tolerable level of discomfort.

- ❏ Prevent constipation by taking a stool softener; drinking water; and eating fruits, vegetables, and whole grains.

❑ Accept anger and depression as normal consequences of weakness, surgery, and stress. Be prepared for good days and bad days.

❑ Try to keep realistic expectations for recovery.

❑ If you feel frustrated because you cannot talk to your surgeon at length, arrange to take up your concerns with another professional.

Chapter Six

RECOVERING AT HOME

Going home—hallelujah! In anticipation of the great day, there's much to learn: what medications you need; how these new medications affect other medications you take from time to time such as aspirin for headaches, antihistamines for allergies, and antacids for indigestion; what you can eat; how you will spend your days; what kind of exercise you can do; what you can't do; when you can travel, go back to work, make love.

As you prepare to cut the umbilical cord of the hospital, there is so much information to assimilate that many hospitals offer discharge classes. In other hospitals, patients receive the information via closed circuit television, booklets, or chats with the patient educator. Regardless of how the information is proffered, patients characteristically feel overwhelmed by a cascade of details they fear they will never remember. That's normal: take notes, turn on a tape recorder, invite the family to sit in, ask questions, repeat the questions. There are too many details for anyone to recall. What's more, just as the stress of the preoperative hours interfered with concentrating and remembering, so the excitement and concerns at the time of discharge shorten the memory and make paying attention difficult. Sensitive nurses, therapists, and physicians realize that you cannot absorb all this information at once, and they are prepared to repeat themselves.

The Theme of Recovery

Regardless of how discharge information is presented, these underlying messages should come through:

Recovery is not yet completed even though discharge from the hospital means that it is well underway. For at least the next few weeks—and maybe for as long as several months—you must remain dedicated to the hard work of recovery. Inherent in those duties are respecting the healing process with its associated discomforts and fatigue, being dedicated to a life-style governed by exercise and rest, and accepting the emotional trials characteristic of this arduous recuperation.

Patients often go home before all infections, irregular heartbeats, or other complications are resolved. Despite continuing difficulties, the very fact that you are being discharged means that the complications are not worrisome and can be managed safely from home.

Although you may have spent many years plagued by angina, you are not a cardiac cripple now. You put up with all the difficulties and discomforts associated with surgery because surgery held the promise for a higher quality of life. Getting on with that life should be your first priority, and continuing the work of recovery your immediate goal.

All patients go home with questions and uncertainties. Understandably, some even fear going home. While they were in the hospital, they could count on skilled professionals to manage any setbacks. Surely, every patient who experienced a sudden arrhythmia that brought the nurses scurrying wonders, "What if it happens at home?"

Because patients routinely go home with unsettling discomforts and continuing need for medical attention, many receive home health services on a daily basis for a short period. To keep watch over patients who were discharged after just 4 or 5 days in the hospital, most surgeons have their patients come to the office a day or two after discharge. A salutary excursion that seems to promote feelings of well-being, this visit also provides an opportunity to have stitches or staples removed (unless the incision was closed with absorbable sutures, which do not require removal). To help patients resolve lingering concerns, many good hospitals and surgeons encourage patients to call a knowledgeable liaison—perhaps a patient educator, a counselor, or an information specialist in the surgeon's office—when concerns arise during the first weeks at home.

"Our patients go home knowing we welcome their calls," said clinical nurse specialist Barbara Friedman. "Usually they call with specific questions, but sometimes they call just to talk. One patient called after he had been home a week to say, 'I had heart surgery and I just realized its significance.' "

This kind of liaison provides security and buffers the transition between hospital and home, especially when patients feel apprehensive because they cannot interpret their discomfort. You must not hesitate to contact this person if you have worries or questions. Resist the inclination to ignore your concerns out of consideration for a medical professional's busy day. Gnawing insecurity can warp your self-confidence. On the contrary, if you resolve your concerns and questions, you will gain confidence and your concerns will diminish. Within a week or so, you will probably feel secure enough that the frequency of your calls will fall off.

Many patients report that their first week at home was more difficult than the last day or so in the hospital. Going home can emphasize patients' weakness and vulnerability, just as moving from the ICU to a regular room had done a few days earlier. One patient, exhausted by the ride home, encountered new pains and felt, for the first time, that he needed help getting into and out of bed.

"I was thrilled to get out of the hospital, but my euphoria didn't last long. The pain really started after I got home," he remembered.

Had this patient regressed? No, he was feeling the intensified pain that normally accompanies fatigue. Although he felt energetic when he got dressed that morning, the trip from the hospital wore him out. In the hospital, when he felt tired he got right into bed and rested. At home, the challenges and the distances were greater. Although his fatigue hit him as he got out of the car, he still had to walk to the house. "The front path never seemed so long," he recalled.

Once inside, he went to lie down and suddenly found that task difficult, too.

"In the hospital, I had worked out this elaborate system of hanging onto the bed rail to ease myself into bed. I'd keep the bed tipped up and, once I was settled, I'd just push the button and adjust the angle to whatever position was comfortable. When I got home, I didn't have those contraptions, and I didn't realize how much I had depended on them. At home, my bed was too low and flat. Getting settled hadn't been so hard since the day after I left the ICU."

Another patient found it jolting to lose the insular quality of the hospital.

"In the hospital, I didn't have to worry about anything," she said. "Every morning, the nurse delivered my menu for the next day and I circled my choices. Then, like clockwork, the trays came and they were picked up. Not at home. My sister brought me home from the hospital and after she helped me get settled, she asked me what we should have for lunch. Lunch? Do I know? I had to think, 'What's in the house? Do I have tuna fish in the cupboard? Is there bread in the freezer? How can we have tuna fish without lettuce and tomatoes? At that moment, it would have been no more difficult to eradicate the national debt."

At home the walk from bed to bathroom is likely to be longer than in the hospital. At home you are expected to shower, shave, and get dressed. While you will probably get up in the morning feeling full of energy, by the time you have accomplished a routine you normally don't give a second thought, half the morning will be gone and you will feel ready for a nap.

"At home, my bed was too low and flat."

"I think the problems seemed worse at home because they were inconsistent with the feelings I associated with home. Resting every other minute in the hospital was normal enough. At home, I'm not accustomed to resting, and having to rest seemed to exaggerate my vulnerability," said a third patient.

"The weakness got to me," still another patient remembered. "For weeks, getting washed in the morning took forever. I had no ambition to do anything, and in the kitchen, I was helpless. I didn't have the strength to slice a carrot or open a can. A month after I was home, I got in the car for the first time to do an errand, and I didn't have enough strength in my arms to turn the wheel. I had to leave the car at the end of the driveway and go inside to call a friend to come and move it. Two weeks later, I was back at work, but I was still tired and needed to rest."

Lingering Discomforts

You can expect a variety of unpleasant feelings after you are discharged. Pain in the incisions, rubbing of the sternum, and numbness in the chest may continue for weeks. Many patients complain of discomfort in their chests for months, especially when the barometer drops. In addition, sleeplessness, lack of appetite, and abdominal distress commonly persist, as do periodic feelings of anxiety, depression, and dependency. Some patients feel dizzy, frequently as a side effect of medication.

Fatigue

For many, the most difficult aspect of recovery is the unique brand of fatigue characteristic of recuperation from surgery, caused in part by anemia.[1] Patients describe this fatigue as a

---

[1]Despite blood-saving strategies in the operating room, heart surgery almost always entails some blood loss. Most physicians do not treat modest blood loss with transfusions, how-

bone-deep weariness that strikes without warning. Although most people perceive a marked increase in stamina after just a week at home, many of these same men and women contend that residual fatigue lingers for at least a year.

"One second I was fine, the next I was too tired," one patient recalled. "And when that exhaustion hit, I was no good for anything. Everything hurt more. My muscles quivered, and my nerves felt raw. It was terrible. I was told to rest before I felt tired, in other words to prevent fatigue. But when you're feeling fine and the fatigue comes without warning, that's hard to do."

That is hard to do, especially if you are impatient about recovering and eager to test your growing strength. Consequently, patients who feel fine typically drain their energy and then succumb to fatigue. For weeks life seems like a seesaw—one moment feeling fine, the next feeling wretched. In spite of steadily increasing levels of energy, every time fatigue and its companion pain hit, they are discouraging. "Will I ever recover?" patients understandably worry. Anticipating fatigue and resting before it strikes will reduce this seesawing and the emotional havoc that accompanies it. If you can rest before you deplete your reservoir of energy, you will avoid untold frustration and demoralization.

Depression and Irritability

Short-lived bouts of depression and irritability are virtually inevitable nevertheless, just as they were in the hospital. Emotional short fuses often accompany physical debilitation. In the first weeks at home, some patients become uncharacteristically dependent and childlike. Some are unable to make decisions as small as which movie to watch on the VCR. Many become unusually tense and sensitive. Intolerant of their own shortcomings and those of others, they can

---

ever, because they can be risky. They prefer to prescribe iron and permit the blood to come back by itself, even though fatigue may be exacerbated in the interim.

be unpleasant and difficult to live with. Little annoyances they normally ignore suddenly exasperate them. "Why are the television commercials so stupid? Damn it, the chicken is overcooked! I wish that neighbor would walk her dog somewhere else."

One patient, who said she had been accustomed to controlling her emotions since she had been a small girl, became angry and tearful after her surgery and stayed that way for months.

"I cried in church and I cried at the supermarket. I cried when I cooked, and I cried when I got into bed at night. I still don't really understand why I got so depressed," she said. "And angry! When my husband came home late, I got angry. When he came home early, I got angry, too. When he was sweet, I yelled at him for patronizing me, and when he wasn't, I cried because I thought he didn't care."

When faced with these feelings, patients sometimes withdraw. Some prefer not to socialize, as if they need to draw a protective shield around themselves so they can regain their strength and self-confidence. During this time they commonly cry with little provocation, although some stoics turn their depression inward because they cannot permit their feelings to show.

"Be patient when your dad gets withdrawn or surly," one former patient advised a young man whose father was about to undergo bypass surgery. "He will have to slow down every facet of his life. It's a difficult adjustment, and he won't be himself for a long time."

Ironically, this advice is particularly valid when it pertains to patients who felt little preoperative fear. Somehow, when patients are afraid beforehand, they have an easier time accepting the lengthy debilitation afterward. Unconsciously they deduce that any procedure which could provoke so much apprehension must be serious enough to require a long and slow recuperation. Patients are also especially vulnerable to bouts of depression and irritability if they feel apprehensive about their well-being.

"I was relentlessly angry at my wife," recalled a patient whose short temper sent him back to the psychotherapist who had discharged him 2 years earlier. "I didn't realize I was really angry at my frailty and bad luck. Why me? What did I ever do to deserve a bad heart?"

Other patients are worried about dying. One asserted, "You're concerned about going through this again in a certain amount of time. You're concerned that even though everything feels fine, something is going to go wrong."

Another patient agreed, "I'm obsessed with the fear of dying." Though his surgery had taken place 3 months before he made this comment, and although he was working full time, he acknowledged that questions about his mortality plagued him constantly.

A third patient put the same concerns slightly differently: "On some level, everyone knows they won't live forever. Since my surgery, though, questions about how well and how long I will live haunt me every day. I can force them to the back of my mind, but I can't make them go away."

While many patients learn to identify the causes of residual aches, some complain that they are forever uncertain. Persistent anxiety sends some back to their physicians repeatedly, and when an electrocardiogram confirms that all is well, they worry someone has made a mistake.

Understandably, when patients feel they are not recovering properly, they become more vulnerable to depression. And unfortunately, a variety of problems can linger or recur.

Memory loss and difficulty concentrating plague many heart surgery patients, sometimes for more than 6 months after they are home. Patients complain they cannot remember what they read, they forget people's names, they get confused easily, they lose their train of thought. Some reveal that, while they are talking, their minds suddenly go blank. Others say their mental processes have simply slowed down.

To some extent, these complaints are common for anyone recovering from major surgery and illness. Separately and in combination with one another, medication, stress, and hardening of the arteries that lead to the brain, all contribute to the problem. Yet, over the years ample evidence has shown that these difficulties can be particularly profound after heart surgery. While the cause is still unclear, the culprit seems to be the heart–lung machine. Some experts suspect that, despite superior technology, tiny air bubbles can pass through the machine's filters and momentarily impede oxygen supply to the brain. Others wonder whether changes in blood pressure, variations in oxygen and carbondioxide levels, and methods for cooling and warming the blood pay a part. Still others theorize that the brain, which normally receives its blood supply in a pulsating fashion, is adversely affected by the steady output of blood from the heart–lung machine. Perhaps the problem emanates from the simple fact that the tubing of the heart–lung machine is different from the lining of natural blood vessels. Whatever the cause, the problem is real. It even has a name: postpump syndrome. But fortunately, it is also on the decline, probably because of recent improvements in the heart–lung machine. And when the problem occurs, it is temporary.

While patients are routinely reassured that their mental faculties will return, many presume the worst nevertheless. "Memory difficulties? I must have had a stroke. Or maybe it's Alzheimer's disease. After all," patients could legitimately reason, "heart surgery can trigger a stroke, and I am at the age when lots of people show the first signs of Alzheimer's disease."

Despite catastrophic expectations, those who have been affected report that their mental difficulties begin to subside after about 6 months, and within a year they are all but gone. Postpump syndrome reflects permanent neurological changes in less than 1% of cases. However, if after 6 months your difficulties with thinking, concentrating, and remembering continue unabated, they may be indicative of depression, according to a 1988 study by British psychologist Stanton Newman.

Dr. Newman tested 60 patients to assess intellectual function and depression. Surprisingly, he discovered that patients who complained of limitation were more likely to be depressed than mentally impaired. Some of those who were actually impaired had no complaints. Conversely, some who were depressed but exhibited no measurable disability were among the group that complained the most. Thus, Dr. Newman concluded that "subjective reports of cognitive function following [bypass surgery] do not reflect actual changes in cognition but rather appear to be sensitive to mood state." These results jibe with our discovery that depression after heart surgery is commonly disguised.

Debilitating though these problems can be, you should not be alarmed by them so long as you begin to see improvement by the time 6 months have passed. While the problems persist, you can compensate by keeping notes and lists. A magnetic pad on the refrigerator, a tiny notebook for purse or pocket, pencils and paper in every room of the house are valuable crutches for two reasons. Most obviously, when ideas (even reminders to call Cousin Nancy or pick up a new drill bit at the hardware store) are committed to paper, they don't get forgotten. In addition, writing notes promotes learning. Just as schoolchildren often practice spelling words by writing them over and over, when you write reminders to yourself, you may help to retrain your memory.

Signs of Serious Depression

Our research revealed that patients recover emotionally at different rates, just as they recover physically at different speeds. Normal reactive depression may peak as late as 3 months after surgery. Almost always, it is a reflection of weakness and debilitation. It wanes decidedly as vigor returns and patients begin to assume more control over their lives.

Some people, however, continue to be plagued by depression in spite of solid physical recovery. Even months after surgery, a few have trouble getting on with life. Some enjoy being invalids. They relish being nursed and pampered. Some who suffered from angina for years become so bound by fear that they are helpless. Some feel too listless to make love, plan an activity, or face the challenges of the day. They may feel estranged from their families, friends, colleagues, even from their former selves. Perhaps they see restaurant menus and television food commercials as ugly reminders of what they should not eat. Possibly they interpret solicitous behavior by friends and colleagues as a measure of their compromised worth. They may become enraged because they feel their family and friends are patronizing.

If you fit any of these descriptions, you may be suffering from long-term debilitating depression. You may also be significantly depressed if you don't feel well and your cardiologist insists that nothing is wrong, or if your difficulties reading, concentrating, and remembering show no signs of letting up.

Profound depression demands attention by a trained mental health professional and, with professional help, can often be alleviated quickly. In the rare instance when patients are depressed because of permanent cardiac disability, psychotherapy can likewise be beneficial. While it cannot change the cardiac health picture, psychotherapy may enable patients to eat better, sleep more soundly, and feel more optimistic about their lives.

Medical Complications

Occasionally, complications do arise or some degree of permanent disability lingers. A 55-year-old veteran of two bypass operations was justifiably disheartened when shortness of breath prevented him from walking any appreciable distance. Another patient, who had recovered steadily for a month, was suddenly beset with postcardiotomy syndrome, characterized by fever, depression, aching, and chest pain

You can compensate by keeping notes and lists.

frighteningly reminiscent of angina. Pleurisy and blood clots can also impede recovery, and occasionally such complications put patients back in the hospital.

Evelyn Samson was recovering slowly but steadily enough to maintain a positive outlook. Then she developed blood clots in her lung, which required her to be rehospitalized.

"You can't imagine how bleak the future looked at that point. Recovery had been hard, but I was staying with it, and then, I was back in the hospital. Oh, good Jesus, I was sure I would never get better," she lamented.

Though Mrs. Samson's clots were dissolved and she was released within a week, the setback was too much for her to cope with, and she found herself unable to shake depression. Her cardiologist recommended short-term psychotherapy, which was effective, and Mrs. Samson was fully recovered, physically as well as emotionally, 8 months later.

Signs of Progress

Eager to put their surgery behind them, many patients assess recovery through tangible signs, literally measuring their progress in footsteps. As they walk farther and faster, they know they're getting better. Some identify progress with the easing of pain. *New York Times* journalist Douglass Cater reported that by the end of 3 weeks virtually all his pain was gone, leaving only residual aches in his rib cage, noticeable primarily at night and early in the morning. Other patients recall that the muscle pain in the shoulder blades subsided, or that the numbness in the chest diminished.

Coping Strategies

In addition to tracking their progress, many patients make a conscious effort to cope. A number of patients find sustenance in God. Some who had always been religious rely heavily on faith. And some who had once rejected religion find themselves drawn to church or synagogue for the first time in many years.

Some patients meditate while others seek solitude on the beach or in the park. Still others rely on internal dialogue. One patient confided, ''When I feel down, I make my intellectual self talk to my emotional self and say, 'You feel bad now, but you won't always feel this way.' Later, or the next day, when I am feeling better, my intellectual self reminds my emotional self, 'See, now you feel better. You might feel bad again, but it won't last.' ''

Many patients attribute their recovery to the understanding and support they received from their families and friends. In a marriage where communication is good and mutual understanding solid, a husband and wife can relieve each other's stresses and grow closer in the process. Not every patient is married and not every marriage is good, however. One single man called upon his only cousin to support him through surgery, and found that their relationship deepened because his cousin felt needed. Another single patient set up a schedule for her friends.

''I was conscious of not overburdening anyone, and I figured that my friends would appreciate specific requests. So I gave everyone an assignment. I always had company when I wanted it, and there was always someone to go to the grocery store or cook dinner.''

Some patients found comfort comparing notes with other patients and, after they recovered, found ongoing strength in peer support groups. After their recovery, several began serving as peer advisers to help other patients through their surgery and recovery.

''It helps to know that other people are feeling what you are feeling,'' one advocate of peer support groups asserted.

While support from others is invaluable, the bulk of the responsibility for recovery lies with you. Inherent in this responsibility is a positive attitude and a commitment to work hard. As Barbara Friedman, clinical nurse specialist, tells her discharge classes, "You may have 10 minutes every day for a pity party. No more. It's self-defeating."

One patient, with a history of cancer, osteoporosis, and more than a dozen major operations, claimed that a positive attitude enabled her to recover from heart surgery despite serious complications.

"I push, that's all." She summarized her feelings this way:

> I get up and I walk even though I know that I'll be in agony when I get home. When I couldn't walk because of leg problems, I rode a stationary bike. Sometimes, I get blue and I cry. "I don't believe it," I tell my husband. "Here's another problem. I'd like to wake up just once and feel fine." So he sits beside me and strokes my back and tells me, "You're entitled." But before you know it he'll remind me of someone who has worse trouble. Then I think, "Well, I survived this," and I feel better.

Several years after her surgery, she still had many medical problems, but she did not dwell on them. "No day is boring. Our travel and activity are limited because of my health," she admitted, "but we always find adventure. We walk in different places, we drive to different destinations, we explore new stores and museums."

Setting a purpose or a goal helped many patients keep a positive attitude during the difficult weeks. One patient planned the retirement he had looked forward to for years. He started painting, made travel plans, and set up a part-time consulting business. Other retired people prepared to invest their energies in a hobby, volunteer work, activities with friends, or organizations. After 6 weeks or so, when they were able to do the activities they planned, they discovered that the diversion took their minds off their bodies and put a better sense of balance back into their lives. For patients who had not yet retired, returning to work was often a panacea. It kept them busy, distracted them from their discomforts, and reaffirmed their sense of worth.

As one patient, who returned to work 4 weeks after surgery, put it, "I don't have time to think about my aches and pains."

In the early weeks of recovery, patients are commonly egocentric and excessively alert to every ache and twinge, but this preoccupation ultimately fades. As the weeks stretch into months and patients feel stronger, most let go of their fixation with their health and mortality. One patient, who had a coronary one September and bypass surgery the following January, returned to his job as a mechanic in July, rejoined his bowling team in August, and bowled his first 200 game of the season in September. Six years later, he was vigorous and active. Although he and his wife remained dedicated members of their hospital's support group, they spent little time ruminating about his well-being.

In these later months, many patients discover that life is better than it has ever been. Many boast their surgery made them appreciate life in a refreshing new way. Some become less driven, more capable of relaxing and enjoying leisure time. Some proclaim they have become motivated less by guilt and obligation, more by desire and genuine interest. Some claim they have learned to live with greater joy; they are more candid and forthright, and they appreciate their loved ones more.

Within a year after surgery—and it may take that long—most patients feel they have changed for the better in some way. Indeed, many patients feel reborn and rejuvenated. Experiencing more than a change in philosophy, these people discover reservoirs of energy that make them feel 10, 20 years younger. They are jubilant to be rid of their angina, to be able to eat, walk, swim, and run without pain. Many claim that, with a new appreciation for their loved ones, their marriages and family lives have improved. Many feel their experience has given them more insight into themselves. Some have acquired greater religious faith.

One patient, celebrating the first anniversary of his bypass, exclaimed how grateful he felt to have had the surgery.

"To think that I'm alive! How lucky I am. I'm fortunate that medical science is as sophisticated as it is. I was lucky to have my surgeon and to have recovered. And now, I'm thrilled because I feel so good."

Points to Remember

❏ Gradually you will grow stronger and more self-confident.

❏ Continue the work of recovery diligently.

❏ Anticipate fatigue and rest before it strikes.

❏ Call your designated medical liaison when you have questions or concerns.

❏ Utilize relaxation techniques, meditation, self-dialogue, and other coping techniques.

❏ Compensate for memory loss by making lists.

❏ Give your family and friends specific requests for help and support.

Chapter Seven

PRESCRIPTION FOR RECOVERY

Recovering from heart surgery requires patience and perseverance. It is aided by breaking down overwhelming problems into smaller, more manageable components; putting depression into perspective; and remembering that, while one day might look bleak, the next is bound to be brighter. This chapter is a manual for this process, with detailed attention to the first weeks. In all instances where these guidelines differ from your physician's instructions, defer to your physician. If you have questions about any of these instructions, talk with your doctor.

Arranging for Help

During at least your first week at home, you should have someone with you most of the time, for many of your tasks will require help. If your spouse works, this first week at home, not the week you were in the hospital, is the best time for her or him to take off. Sometimes spouses, particularly husbands, feel threatened by this kind of responsibility. If so, call on someone else. If you live alone, you'll need someone to stay with you as well. Perhaps a friend or grown son or daughter would be willing to give you a hand. If your only choice is a married child with a family of his or her own who lives in a distant city, consider imposing. Having your son or daughter with you will solve your practical problems. In addition, it might give you the opportunity for a uniquely meaningful visit. In the atmosphere of recovery, where you need assistance and your child can meet your needs, new, long-lasting bonds often form. At the end of the week, when it's time to say good-bye, you are likely to discover your relationship has strengthened, your closeness deepened.

In any one of a number of circumstances, you may find yourself needing the help of strangers. Maybe your spouse is uncomfortable or needs help taking care of you. Perhaps you live alone and have absolutely no one you feel comfortable calling on. Whatever the reason, patients sometimes discover they need to find someone who can take care of them temporarily. Alternatively, they sometimes need someone to do the marketing and cooking or someone to help with banking and bill paying or someone to drive them to the physician's office. Depending upon your personal situation and geographic location, a number of alternatives exist.

Under some limited circumstances, homemaker and personal care services are covered by private health insurance, by Medicare Part B, and by Medicaid. In addition, federal legislation called the Older Americans Act mandates that services like home delivered meals, assistance with housekeeping and personal care, friendly visitors, and telephone reassurance be available for free or at nominal cost to all frail people over age 60 as well as to disabled people of any age. It is only fair to note, however, that the quality of services varies greatly from location to location. To find out availability in your area and your personal eligibility, check with the social services department at your local hospital or with your Area Agency on Aging.

Because the need for service is great, availability spotty, and insurance coverage very limited, bartering guilds are burgeoning to offer people a clearinghouse for exchanging services. Through a service cooperative you could arrange, for example, to have a volunteer go grocery shopping for you during your recuperation in exchange for your volunteering to drive someone to the doctor after you recuperate. There are some 75 service credit banks operating nationwide, with another 20 or so in some planning stage. To learn more about cooperative service organizations and obtain a directory of existing programs, write to Kathleen Treat, Service Credit Program, Center on Aging, Room 1240 HHP

Building, University of Maryland, College Park, Maryland 20742-2611.

When people can afford to, however, they usually prefer to hire help, and in most hospitals, the social service or nursing department is prepared to help you make the necessary contacts or arrangements. They will help you assess your needs and find people to meet them. If your hospital cannot provide this assistance, you can get it from independent professional care managers.

As families have grown more distant geographically and increasing numbers of women have returned to the work force, this surrogate support system has emerged to provide varied forms of assistance to the ill and the elderly. Typically, these professionals are social workers. Like many hospital-based social workers, they meet with their clients (or their clients' grown children), help them assess their needs, and help find the appropriate caregivers to meet those needs for as long as is necessary. They also supervise to make sure everything is going well.

This service burgeoned when aging family members needed help but their grown children could not provide it personally. Often, the children live in a distant city and work with a social worker in their hometown. This social worker then connects the clients with a colleague in the city where their parent lives, and an effective network of support and communication develops. But the service is highly individualized. It is available to younger people who have temporary needs as well as to aged people with permanent needs. If you live alone and feel uneasy about the possibility of becoming ill at night, a care manager might arrange a personal emergency response system. These can be rented for about $50.00 a month. If you need someone to help with housework until you're strong enough to take over again, a manager can arrange that, too.

Ordinarily, care managers charge for their services, although under some circumstances financial subsidy is available. To learn more about this kind of assistance, contact your Area Agency on Aging or the National Council on the Aging. You can also obtain a referral at no charge by calling the National Association of Professional Care Managers, (602) 881-8008. This organization, comprising nurses, social workers, and other professionals specializing in geriatric care management, grants membership in several categories (associate, professional, advanced professional, and fellow). Fellows are board certified and carry the organization's highest credentials.

Clothing

For the trip home and for the next couple of weeks, choose clothing that is easy to put on and comfortable to wear. Women often find that wearing a bra, even for sleeping, helps keep their breasts from pulling against their incisions. Some women prefer front-closing bras because they are easier to fasten, while others choose bras that close in the back because they are less irritating to the healing scar. Men sometimes complain that button-down shirts irritate their scars as does the hair growing in on their chests. Patients who have been particularly bothered by their healing incisions have devised a variety of ingenious contraptions to protect them. Some have tried dry gauze bandages, though men readily admit that putting tape onto the itchy stubble of new chest hair is less than satisfactory. Some have experimented with thin sanitary napkins, which they stick to their clothing. Try using one pad over the scar as a bandage. Alternatively, affix one paid on either side of the scar to form a protective channel. Sometimes women, as well as men, find comfort in a plain cotton T-shirt worn as an undershirt. Most patients simply opt for pullover shirts in a soft fabric.

Beyond comfort, appearance matters, not for visitors but for you. Looking good will help lift your mood while it subtly reminds you that, although you are newly home from the hospital, you are not sick; you are recovering from surgery. Choose attractive clothing in appealing colors. Men, shave every day and splash on your favorite aftershave cologne. Women, if you enjoy wearing makeup, put in on every day. If you get your hair washed and set, arrange for someone to do that for you soon after you come home. If you blow your hair dry, arrange for someone to help you as often as your normally wash your hair. Alloting extra time and making special arrangements are well worth the trouble. If you ask friends and relatives to help you with these and other specific tasks, they will probably be grateful; knowing how they can help you will make them feel wanted and needed.

Support Stockings

At most hospitals, patients are outfitted with support stockings to stimulate circulation in the legs. Continue to wear your support stockings for 2 to 3 weeks at home. You may take these off to sleep at night and to bathe, but they should be put on before you get out of bed in the morning. You'll need help with this task. It's a struggle, and your incision has not healed enough for you to manage it alone.

To support your legs properly, your elastic stockings must lie smoothly. Wrinkles act as rubber bands and will cut off your circulation. To help your elastic stockings do their job, keep your legs elevated whenever you are sitting, and remember not to cross your legs.

Activity Schedule

For at least 3 to 4 weeks following your discharge, recuperation will be a full-time job. By balancing activity and rest, you can fill the entire day. Like any job, recuperation has its challenges and its drudgery. It includes work that is best done alone and work that benefits from team cooperation.

Remember that, although 5 weeks can feel like an eternity, especially when those weeks are marked by discomforts and depression, this period will end. Your strength will return. You will feel better. In the meantime, respect disability.

If you go to bed and try to sleep more than once during the day, you will probably have greater difficulty sleeping at night. Try to get as many of hours sleep at night as you normally do. If you find you must stay up late one night, try to nap earlier in the day. Force yourself to exercise despite lethargy. Getting up and getting going will help raise your spirits and spark some energy.

Day of Discharge

When you get home from the hospital, you will probably be so tired that you will want to lie down. Even if you don't feel tired, rest for an hour when you first get home. Then resume whatever schedule you were following your last day or so in the hospital.

First Week at Home

Take pain medications according to your discharge instructions. Applying moist heat will also relieve pain. If you can, use an electric fomentation unit (brand name Thermophore), a heating pad designed to create moist heat by utilizing the moisture in your body. If you don't have one and can't obtain one, use a damp towel beneath a heating pad shielded with a heat-resistant plastic cover. You'll need help wetting the towel and wringing it out. If you attempt this task yourself, you will strain your chest incision, so ask someone else to do it for you.

If you are taking medicine for pain, plan to begin exercising 45 minutes to an hour after taking your pill. Continue your physical therapy exercises once a day. Do your breathing exercises four times a day. Walk in the house four times a day. It's important to cool down after exercise so your heart rate slows gradually. To cool down, breathe slowly and deeply. While sitting down, point your toes then flex your feet 10 times. Bend your knees and straighten your legs 10 times. Rest before showering.

Since exercising and eating tax the heart, you should rest for one hour after meals and half an hour between activities, preferably not in bed. A recliner is ideal. If you don't have one and can't borrow one, try a comfortable lounge chair or couch. Remember, however, that the lower and flatter you put yourself, the harder it will be to get up and down independently.

The bone incision in your chest, like a broken bone, takes 5 weeks to heal. During this time, do not lift or push anything that weighs more than 10 to 15 pounds. Do not drive the car, vacuum, mow the lawn, move furniture, lift a baby, carry groceries or suitcases, or reach for objects on a shelf above your head. In addition, do not try to unscrew a stubborn jar, open a sticking window, or perform any other task that requires a similar struggle. Activities like these will keep your chest incision from healing.

To make yourself more self-sufficient in the kitchen, have someone move dishes and glasses so that they are no higher than shoulder level. In addition, unstack pots and pans so you don't have to lift a heavy pile in order to get to the one on the bottom.

When you first get home, everything you do will take longer than usual. Showering, dressing, eating, exercising, and resting will consume nearly the entire day. By the end of the first week at home, a typical day might look like this:

8:00 Wake up, get help putting on elastic stockings, wash, and have breakfast
8:30 Rest with a morning TV show; do breathing exercises
9:30 Shower, get help with elastic stockings
9:45 Rest with the morning newspaper
10:15 Shave or put on your makeup; get dressed

10:45 Rest with Duke Ellington; do breathing exercises

11:15 Physical therapy

12:00 Lunch

12:30 Rest with the afternoon news; perhaps you'll doze

2:30 Walk; cool down

3:30 Rest with Agatha Christie; do breathing exercises

4:00 Entertain guests for one hour

5:00 Rest with the National Geographic

5:30 Prepare a martini and make the salad for dinner

6:00 Dinner

6:30 Rest with the evening news; do breathing exercises

7:30 Play a round of poker with some friends

9:30 Bed; remove elastic stockings

Some patients complain that recovery is unbearably monotonous. If you use your resting time creatively, it is likely to seem less dreary. Take advantage of this time to think through home repair projects you've been planning for years, dictate letters to your secretary, study new cookbooks, and learn the principles of good nutrition, get on the phone and make contact with a friend whom you haven't spoken to in months. As time goes on, the length of your activities will increase, and you will need to rest fewer times each day.

Second Week at Home

Continue resting one hour after each meal, half an hour after each activity. Continue breathing exercises four times a day and physical therapy once a day.

You may take walks outside now when the weather is mild. Be careful to keep your incision covered; sunlight will damage this tender new skin. Begin with no more than one block once a day. Remember, however far you walk away from home, you must return the same distance, and fatigue often strikes without warning. Test your stamina and increase your distance gradually. By the end of this week, you should be doing four blocks (two blocks each way) or one-fourth of a mile. Choose flat terrain. In the summer, walk in the evening or early in the morning to avoid intense heat and sun. In the winter, choose the middle of the day to avoid extreme cold or wind. Since hills, wind, heat, cold, and sun make the heart work harder, you may have to continue walking indoors for a second week. Alternatively, you can spend your exercise time riding a stationary bicycle at low tension. Try reading a book, watching television, or listening to music while you ride to help pass the time. Under no circumstances is inclement weather an excuse not to exercise. Continue cool-down exercises, and rest before showering. If exercise produces pain, stop, rest, and consult your doctor.

Always take and record your pulse before walking and exercising, then again immediately upon finishing. Pressing lightly but firmly with your index and middle fingers, find the radial artery on the palm side of your wrist. Never use your thumb to take your pulse since the thumb also has a pulse, which can confuse your count. Count the number of beats for 6 seconds, then add a zero to your number to determine your heart rate for one minute. If you have trouble finding your pulse, you can purchase a mechanical pulse meter, sold at sporting goods stores. These vary in design, capability, accuracy, and price, beginning at about $70.

Your heart rate during exercise should be at least 10 beats per minute higher than your resting heart rate but no higher than 120. Use your pulse rate as a guide for increasing your workout; if your heart rate rises more than 30 beats per minute, do not increase the duration and vigor of your regime. As your stamina increases, your present routine will raise your heart rate less. When your exercising heart rate rises less than 30 beats per minute, you can safely increase your challenges.

Your pulse should return to its resting rate within 15 minutes of finishing your workout. If it exceeds 120 during exercise or fails to slow sufficiently within 15 minutes, consult your doctor.

This week and always, try to set a consistent time each day for exercising. Doing so will help put structure in your day and ensure that the day doesn't slip by without this all-important activity. Use good judgment to strike a healthy balance between increasing your activity level and avoiding fatigue.

This week you may begin to climb stairs. Take them slowly and remember to breathe deeply. Resist the inclination to hold your breath (see section on physical therapy exercises below).

You may take short car rides as a passenger, get your hair cut, visit your favorite hardware store. (Be sure to wear your seat belt even if you are going only to the corner drug store; a minor accident could ram you into the dashboard and injure your healing breastbone.)

During inclement weather, consider riding to a local mall for your walks. Increasingly, malls are opening their corridors half an hour or so before the stores open so walkers can get their exercise. Don't forget to cool down. Try walking with a friend, then stopping for a cup of tea or a glass of juice to rest up before the car ride home.

Third Week at Home

Continue to rest for one hour after meals and for 30 minutes between activities. Continue physical therapy, breathing exercises, and walking. Don't forget to cool down and rest before showering. By the end of this week, you should be up to 8 to 12 blocks. During this week, you may go out to dinner with friends, take in a movie, plan other short adventures.

If your legs are not swollen, you may stop wearing your elastic stockings.

You may also resume sexual intercourse (see section on sex below).

This week you should begin to massage your chest incision with lotion (see section on bathing and caring for your incision below).

Fourth Week at Home

Continue to rest for one hour after meals and half an hour between activities. You may stop your breathing exercises after this week, but continue your physical therapy and increase your walking up to 16 to 20 blocks, or one mile. You may return to work part time. With the exception of strenuous exertion, resume all normal activities.

With your physician's approval, you may be able to start driving this week. Since you may still be weaker than you think and your reflexes may still be slower than normal, test your mettle cautiously. At first, take short trips on quiet streets free from heavy traffic. For the first several times you drive, have someone in the passenger's seat who can take the wheel if you feel tired.

If a hospital in your area offers a cardiac rehabilitation program, this might be the week for you to begin. For the first couple of months, you should attend three times a week.

Fifth Week at Home

Continue to rest for one hour after meals and half an hour between activities. Continue your physical therapy and increase the distance you are walking until you reach 40 blocks, or 2 miles. Dedicate yourself to walking 2 miles or doing a comparable aerobic exercise every day for the rest of your life. If you find exercise boring, plan to do it with a friend. Call your peer support group (see section on peer support groups below) and get a buddy. Plan different walks each day. Explore the new housing development, a different shopping mall, the local parks.

With your physician's permission, you may return to work full time.

Continue to increase your activities gradually. Continue to anticipate fatigue, and rest before it strikes. Even in the coming months, avoid booking social engagements on heavy business days. Avoid heavy meals. Strive for moderation. Remember, recovery may take a full year.

Physical Therapy Exercises

Physical therapy exercises prevent circulatory disorders, increase mobility, and help improve stamina. In many hospitals, physical therapists work individually with patients on a daily basis, gradually increasing the patients' physical challenges. Before patients are discharged, their physical therapists give them a regimen of exercises, together with suggestions and admonitions, to follow at home.

If you received a physical therapy regime, follow it. Otherwise you might try this one, building your tolerance gradually. Do these exercises once a day at least one hour after eating or half an hour after a preceding activity. If angina occurs during exercise, stop and rest for 15 minutes. If the angina continues, call your doctor. When you exercise, be careful not to hold your breath or you will prevent the exchange of carbon dioxide for oxygen when you need it most. Counting out loud will keep you breathing in spite of the instinctive tendency not to.

1. Lying face up on a bed (the floor is too hard), slide one leg out to the side, and slide it back. Do the same with the other leg. Repeat the pattern four more times.

2. Lying face up on the bed with your arms at your side, raise one arm and reach over your head. Bring your arm back to your side. Then do the same with the other arm. Repeat this pattern four more times.

If you find exercise boring, plan to do it with a friend.

3. Lying in the same position, raise one knee as close to your chest as possible. At the same time, reach for your knee with both hands. Return to the starting position and do the same exercise lifting the other knee. Repeat this sequence four more times.

4. Sitting on the edge of the bed and supporting yourself with both hands behind you, straighten one leg, then return to the original position. Then do the same with the other leg. Repeat the pattern four more times.

5. Sitting on the edge of the bed, make a fist and bend both arms toward your chest as though you were going to beat your chest. Working one arm at a time, straighten your elbow and extend your arm out to the side. Return it to the original position. Repeat the sequence five times with each arm.

6. Sitting on the edge of the bed, resume the original position of the preceding exercise. Twist from the waist up as far to the left as possible. Repeat the movement 10 times. Then twist to the right 10 times.

7. Standing on the floor and supporting yourself against the wall if necessary, rock onto your tiptoes and then back down. Begin with 10 repetitions, and when that feels easy, increase by two repetitions every 3 to 4 days.

8. Standing up and supporting yourself comfortably, bend your knees gently, then return to a straight-leg position. Follow the repetition instructions in the last exercise.

9. Perform the trunk twist described above but in a standing position. Follow the repetition instructions in the preceding exercise.

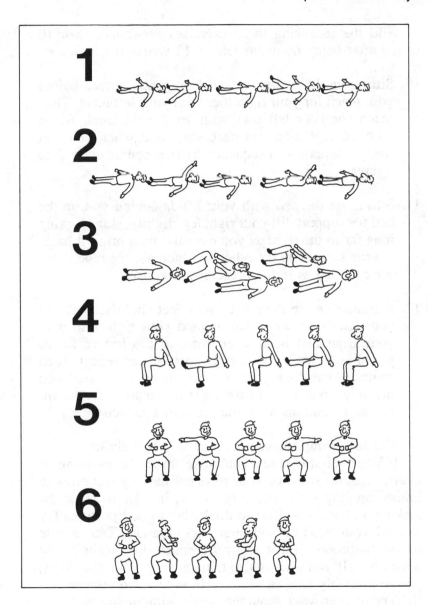

Add the following three exercises no sooner than 10 weeks after being home, as late as 12 weeks if necessary:

10. Sitting on the bed with your legs gently spread before you, reach for your right toes with your left hand. Then reach for your left toes with your right hand. Begin with 10 repetitions on each side, and when you feel ready, increase this sequence by two counts every 3 to 4 days.

11. Sitting on the bed with your hands behind you on the bed for support, lift your right leg slightly, slowly swing it as far to the right as you can, and then bring it back. Do the same with the other leg. Increase the repetitions for each leg as in the preceding exercise.

12. Standing on the floor with your feet slightly apart and your hands on your hips, extend your right arm over your head and bend your trunk to the left as far as possible. Return to an upright position and repeat. Then switch, extending your left arm over your head and bending your trunk to the right as far as possible. Increase repetitions as in the preceding exercise.

The following suggestions may also be helpful:

If you feel stiff when you wake up in the morning or after a nap, do some of your physical therapy exercises to limber up. Fight the postsurgical inclination to stoop by making a conscious effort to think about good posture. Try to hold your head up and your back straight. Tape a note on the bathroom mirror and refrigerator door to help you remember. If you find you're hunching up your shoulders, you're probably tensing muscles in your torso unnecessarily. Try to keep your shoulders loose without stooping forward. If the surgery has confused your muscle memory and you can't tell whether you're standing straight, check your posture in the mirror.

Remember, the speed at which patients are ready to take on new activities varies from patient to patient, and younger people usually progress more rapidly than those who are aged or in poor health. As you get stronger, if you have always been athletic, you should talk to your physician about when you can resume sports. If exercise is new to you, there is a vast world of fitness for you to discover. You need to learn the differences between exercises to protect your heart from further destruction and exercising to achieve optimum cardiac fitness. In addition to cardiovascular exercise, you should also explore strength and flexibility training, which are equally important for protecting health and vitality. What exercise goals are right for you, considering your health and your interests? Whether you're a veteran at exercise or new to the game, you need to know when and to what degree you should intensify your workout. What should your target heart rate be? How long should you sustain your target heart rate and what should your resting heart rate be? If you have a clear understanding of your exercise goals and how to achieve them, you can work out a regime that is emotionally satisfying as well as physically therapeutic.

Drugs

It is important to know what drugs you take, what each one does, what its potential side effects and dangers are, and what precautions to take to avert them. You should go over your medications with your physician, and in addition to the above information, obtain the answers to the following questions.

When should I take this drug? On an empty stomach? In the middle of a meal? After eating? What should I do if I miss a dose?

What should I do if I can't remember when I took the last dose?

*Is there any food, beverage, or other drug I should be
sure to have because of this medication?* For example,
since diuretics tend to deplete the body of potassium,
patients who take drugs such as Lasix (Hoechst-Roussel)
must often make a conscious effort to eat a potassium-
rich diet (including such foods as bananas, oranges, and
broccoli), and sometimes they need to take supplemental potassium.

*Is this drug incompatible with any food, beverage, or
other medication I take?* For example, Coumadin (Du-
Pont), an anticoagulant, is incompatible with aspirin as
well as other drugs commonly prescribed for arthritis.
It is also incompatible with alcohol. Be sure to tell your
physician about all over-the-counter and prescription
drugs you took even occasionally before surgery. Don't
forget to include such routine medications as deconges-
tants, antihistamines, antacids, analgesics, or sleep aids.

*Will this drug interfere with my ability to drive or oper-
ate machinery?*

*Can this drug induce depression, loss of interest in sex-
ual activity, or sexual impotence as a side effect?*

Keep a chart of your medications posted in the kitchen
or bathroom and diligently note when you take each one.
This will help you keep track until your medication schedule
becomes routine.

Remember that each person metabolizes drugs and re-
acts to them individually. Balancing medications effectively
is often a matter of trial-and-error, and it may take some
juggling before your physician finds the best combination
of drugs in the ideal dosages for you. Since adjustments
may need to be made, pay attention to your reactions. Also,
tell your physician about any new feelings that develop,
even if you don't think they are drug-related. Do not stop

taking any medication because you think it's causing a problem. If you have any questions or concerns, consult your physician.

Bathing and Caring for Your Incision

You may begin to shower 24 hours after you return home, even if you still have stitches or staples. Showering, you may discover, is tiring. Avoid steamy hot showers as they will strain your heart and drain your energy. At least at first, it's a good idea to have a stool in the shower so you can sit. Have your spouse or someone else nearby so you can call for help if you feel tired.

Keep soap off your incision for the first 3 days. Sit on the toilet seat cover or a hamper to dry yourself. Pat your incision dry. Plan to rest before shaving, putting on your makeup, or getting dressed.

Caring for your incision will help to relieve itching and minimize the width of your scar. If butterfly bandages were placed across your incision, you may remove them in 3 days. Beginning with the third week you are home, massage your chest in the following manner:

Coat your hands with skin lotion or baby oil. Place one hand on either side of your incision and gently massage the skin beside the incision in circles toward the incision. Repeat this practice four times a day.

Two weeks later, add circles away from your incision. Now you are massaging both toward the incision and away from it four or five times a day.

Another 2 weeks later, begin massaging directly over the incision. Keep up these massages four or five times a day for at least 3 months.

Pay attention to your incision as you massage it or shower. If you notice any new fluid draining from your incision or if it appears newly red or swollen, call your doctor. You should also be alert for other signs of infection, namely fever, increased sensitivity, or heat at the site of the incision. Remember that some discomfort emanating from the incision is normal and may continue for more than a year.

Cardiac Rehabilitation

Attending cardiac rehabilitation, where heart function is carefully monitored and exercise supervised by physical therapists, is an excellent way to develop good exercise habits in the wake of surgery. People worried about the dangers of overexertion find invaluable reassurance in exercising under the vigilant supervision of physical therapists and electronic monitors. In addition, cardiac rehab offers all the benefits of social contact and peer support—critical ingredients, some say, for making exercise enjoyable and establishing good habits they will practice for life. Patients commonly go so far as to credit cardiac rehab with the success of their recovery. Without the heart monitors and reassurance from the professional staff, they contend, they never would have overcome their fears and have been able to put the heart surgery behind them. In addition, cardiac rehab provides an invaluable opportunity to get information and encouragement from staff, to share ''war stories'' and coping strategies with other patients, and thus to put their surgery in perspective.

Research has repeatedly demonstrated that depression and anxiety put people with heart disease at risk for future heart attacks. Cardiac rehab can reduce depression and help patients recapture optimum quality of life, according to two studies presented at the American Heart Association scientific meetings in November 1994. Although this research suggests that, by preventing future cardiac catastrophes and the costs that go with them, cardiac rehab might well be cost effective, earlier research has demonstrated that cardiac rehabilitation is unlikely to make a difference between life and death except for those at especially high risk. This research, which looked only at medical outcome, ignored the emotional fallout of heart surgery. Nevertheless, on the basis of this research, some health insurance policies have sharply curtailed their cardiac rehab allowances. If your insurance refuses to reimburse for cardiac rehabilitation and you can afford to pay for it out-of-pocket, you would be wise to consider doing so.

Insomnia

Patients commonly complain that they have difficulty sleeping for several weeks after surgery. If you have trouble, eliminate caffeine from your diet. Eliminate alcohol as well; although alcohol has the tendency to induce sleepiness initially, its long-term effects disrupt sleep. Avoid napping during the day; make an effort to go to bed at the same time every night and get up early in the morning.

Many patients find establishing a bedtime ritual helps to turn off the mind and prepare it for sleep. One patient began his sequence at 11 every night. He took a warm bath, drank a cup of decaffeinated tea, got into bed, read his favorite psalm, turned on a relaxation tape, and before too many nights had passed, discovered he was asleep before the tape finished. Although the warm bath, hot tea, prayer, and soothing tape may have helped to relax him, the consistency of the ritual was probably the most important ingredient. If you like classical music, incorporate it into your ritual. If you like hot milk, that's fine, too. But so are apples and club soda, so long as you have them every night.

If insomnia persists, discuss it with your physician. Your problem may be medical, and your physician may want to treat it with medication. But before you resort to sleeping pills unnecessarily, try the suggestions above. They can't hurt, and they just might solve the problem.

Diet

In the early days and weeks after surgery, don't be surprised if your taste for food is gone. Anesthesia and medications can make food taste unduly salty, unpleasantly sweet, downright unpalatable. Unless you are in heart failure or have another medical reason for being on a very low-salt diet, you can eat whatever you please until your appetite comes back, so long as you maintain a well-balanced, nutritious diet.

Once your appetite returns, however, it's time to reduce salt and fats, increase fiber, and possibly eat more complex carbohydrates and less protein than you are accustomed to. For people used to bacon and eggs for breakfast every morning or vegetables drenched in butter at dinner every night, this is the moment of dread. The prohibitions all but scream out: no hotdogs, no cream cheese, no cookies, no potato chips. "I'll never eat chocolate cake again," many lament. Others worry that, since they are on a restricted diet, no one will invite them to dinner anymore or that they will have to forego eating out.

It's true that for many patients a heart-healthy diet represents a dramatic change. And when this change threatens to make food unappealing or unsatisfying, it can seem like a terrible punishment. Understandably so.

For most men, women, and children, food is a powerful part of life. From earliest infancy, they learned that food can eradicate their pain and make them feel loved. More than mere sustenance, food carries heavy sensual and emotional overtones. People commonly ease their anguish, reward their successes, salute their triumphs, and celebrate their joys with food. Food is central to every social, emotional, and cultural event we experience. What's a movie without popcorn? A baseball game without a hotdog and beer? A romance without a cozy, candlelight dinner for two?

Because food plays such a pervasive role in life, the psychological impact of a restricted diet can be enormous, but it doesn't have to be adverse. There are millions of life-loving, food-loving people who have discovered low-fat fare and will testify that a healthier diet need not mean deprivation.

A number of converts to low-fat eating, eager to share their enthusiasm, have written creative, innovative cookbooks on the subject. We recommend a few in "Some Additional Resources" at the back of this book, and you'll find a wide selection of others at your local bookstore or public library. Increasingly, food sections of newspapers, women's magazines, and gourmet publications are running regular columns featuring heart-healthy cooking techniques and recipes. In addition, there is a proliferation of magazines dedicated to healthy living, many of which highlight food preparation and presentation.

Whether you're interested in cooking or buying food already prepared, eating healthfully has never been easier. As more and more people have demanded foods lower in fats and sodium, the marketplace has responded. From the freezer to the dairy case to the open shelves, reduced fat and sodium selections abound. Restaurants, too, have met the demand. Many feature dishes made in compliance with American Heart Association guidelines; these are usually clearly marked on the menu for easy identification. Restaurants that don't feature omelets made with egg substitutes or other special dishes are usually happy to answer questions about how their menu items are prepared and to meet requests for steamed vegetables or fish broiled without butter.

Even purveyors of fast food are heeding the call. Thanks largely to pressure exerted by the Center for Science in the Public Interest, you can order 1% milk at McDonald's; salads and baked potatoes at Wendy's; sugar-free, nonfat frozen yogurt at TCBY; bagels at Dunkin' Donuts; a grilled chicken sandwich at Burger King and Hardee's; baked fish and a baked potato at Long John Silver's. You can also order a booklet revealing nutritional information from most fast food organizations. And new franchises featuring chicken barbecued without fat and heart-healthy side dishes are burgeoning.

But beware. In an attempt to lure the health-conscious consumer, food merchants and advertisers have adopted some misleading tactics. Typically, fast food chains offer fried chicken and fish, which hold more fat than their red-meat counterparts. Half-a-dozen chicken nuggets, for example, contain 20 grams of fat while a hamburger may have just 13 grams.

If healthy eating is new to you, you'll have to take the time to get educated. For starters, we recommend an article entitled "Forget about Cholesterol?" published in the March 1990 issue of *Consumer Reports.* In addition, Tufts University publishes a monthly nutrition newsletter. Articles on the latest findings and controversies appear regularly in newspapers and magazines.

To modify your diet without feeling deprived or punished, try approaching your new eating plan as a challenge, looking for healthier ways to prepare your favorite foods and intriguing new dishes. If you're a fried chicken and potatoes fan, roll skin-free chicken pieces in potato buds, coat the pan and the chicken with a cooking oil spray (such as Pam), and bake. If you enjoy exotic fare, explore cookbooks to uncover recipes that call for little fat or that you can successfully modify. In the *Silver Palate Cookbook* by Julie Rosso and Sheila Lukins, for example, you'll find zesty, spicy Pasta Raphael, a sauce featuring fresh tomatoes and marinated artichoke hearts. *The Frog/Commissary Cookbook* by Steven Poses et al., offers a spectacular Japanese swordfish marinade made from combining soy sauce (use the reduced sodium variety), saki, lime juice, and fresh ginger. Even Julia Child, who still embraces butter with passion, provides some options. Her poached peaches with raspberry sauce, found in *Mastering the Art of French Cooking,* make a satisfying and attractive dessert. Because the diet dilemma can so easily entrap people in self-pity, those who have discovered the secrets of enjoyable low-fat dining feel more than satisfied; they feel triumphant. But for everyone who accepts the change with equanimity, there is the fool who cheats at every chance. For everyone who has a positive experience, there is the malcontent who grumbles he has nothing decent to eat.

By the same token, many spouses have assumed the culinary challenge as an expression of commitment and support. But for every spouse who works creatively at making low-fat dishes look and taste appealing, there is another who refuses to learn the tricks because she (or he) contends that a dish without butter is a dish without taste. And for every mate whose creative effort is an expression of love, there is one whose resistance is an expression of anger and sabotage.

If you or your mate have trouble adjusting to a low-fat diet, perhaps you need to look inward. Are you angry at yourself or your mate or heart disease? Do you feel that heart disease is, in some way, a reflection of failure and that punishment is in order? If you can identify the cause of your resistance, perhaps you can overcome it.

Whether you feel resistant or not, these tips can give you a head start toward discovering that healthful eating can be satisfying.

Think Creativity

How many ways are there to prepare fish or chicken? You'd be amazed! Set yourself the goal of trying one new recipe each week, and before long you'll be eating more adventurously as well as more healthfully. If you grow tried of chicken, prepare a turkey breast. Rather than seasoning as you usually do, mix up a marinade made from orange marmalade, the grated rind of an orange, pepper, garlic, ginger, and a small amount of low-sodium soy sauce. Marinate the turkey breast overnight. Bake it; better yet, cook it in the microwave, then brown it under the broiler. You'll have a succulent turkey breast with a subtle but penetrating orange flavor. If you like it, experiment with other marinades for chicken, turkey, and fish. Play with tomato juice mixed with Italian spices—thyme, oregano, and basil. Try soups, wines, and brandy as marinade bases. Get to know curry, cardamom, and cumin. Learn to stir-fry. Explore beans and grains; discover couscous, bulgur wheat, brown rice, and kasha. Make a thick, meatless marinara sauce using canned tomatoes, tomato paste, and tomato sauce, finely chopped onion, garlic, mushrooms, green pepper, celery, and carrots; season with lots of Italian herbs. Keep on the lookout for interesting meatless entrees and for pasta, risoto, and vegetable main dishes that incorporate cheese or other animal protein as secondary ingredients.

Think Substitution

You can often lower the fat content of recipes without sacrificing flavor. Instead of browning chicken in a frying pan, do it under the broiler using no fat whatsoever, then complete the cooking by baking in a cooler oven, microwaving, or simmering. Cut way back on the amount of fat you use to sauté. Instead, choose a nonstick pan and coat it with a cooking oil spray. If necessary, add additional oil (monounsaturated olive oil or canola oil or polyunsaturated safflower oil) by the teaspoon or, better yet, a small amount of wine, flavored vinegar, or defatted chicken broth. (Store unopened cans of chicken broth in the refrigerator. The fat will congeal and rise to the top, so you can easily lift it off.) In salad dressings, replace at least half the oil with water or simply season salads with freshly ground pepper and a splash of flavored vinegar (try raspberry, blueberry, tarragon, sherry, and champagne flavors, for example).

To make a white sauce, use oils low in saturated fat and skim milk instead of butter and cream. For gravy, thicken defatted drippings (place the drippings in the freezer to make the fat congeal) with cornstarch mixed with water. Select ground turkey instead of ground beef. Use lite salt, which has between ⅓ and ½ less sodium than regular table salt, depending on the brand. Rely on low-fat cheeses such as part-skim milk mozzarella. Substitute nonfat yogurt or nonfat sour cream for sour cream and evaporated skim milk for heavy cream; in cooked foods particularly you're unlikely to notice the difference. Opt for low-fat mayonnaise and try butter-flavor substitutes such as Molly McButter on vegetables and potatoes. (If you select garden fresh vegetables and steam them lightly, you may find they are so flavorful that they need no enhancement.) Since crackers are often laden with saturated fats, notably tropical oils, try matzoh, which contains no fat at all, or nonfat crackers instead.

Grow accustomed to less salty tastes by reducing salt and other salty ingredients gradually while compensating with a greater abundance of herbs and other spices. Discover the fragrance and full flavor of fresh herbs, which are readily available in supermarket produce sections. If you use dried herbs and spices, store them in the freezer, where they will retain their zest indefinitely.

Replace caffeinated drinks with decaffeinated equivalents. Since caffeine stimulates the heart, drink no more than three cups of regular coffee, tea, or cola a day.

Think Adventure

Many cuisines, notably some of the Asian ones, are inherently low in fat. Try a Thai or Japanese restaurant. Visit a pasta restaurant or a cafe specializing in new American fare, which characteristically replaces heavy sauces with unusual and interesting combinations of light, fresh ingredients. Since the most interesting selections in many restaurants are served as appetizers, make a meal out of several and forego the main course altogether; choose a salad, several vegetable creations, and perhaps one dish featuring animal protein.

Think Contribution

If you sense you're being overlooked on the dinner-party circuit, suggest that a good friend host a potluck supper, where everyone brings something to share. If you bring a sufficient quantity of a delicious low-fat dish, everyone can partake and no one will look like an outcast. While your discretion may guide you away from some of the choices, you will certainly be able to enjoy others.

Think Festivity

You're well, and you deserve to celebrate. Take out the good silver and china. Enjoy some wine in a delicate stemmed glass. (Unless you are taking blood thinners or your doctor says otherwise, you may have up to 2 ounces of hard liquor or 3 ounces of sweet wine or 5 ounces of dry wine or 10 ounces of beer a day). Have a picnic. Dine with friends.

Think Moderation

In an attempt to lower their cholesterol, countless people changed their diets radically and abruptly. They stopped eating all red meat, they spent hours in the supermarket studying labels, they avoided restaurants for fear of hidden fats. But pretty soon, they got tired of working so hard, they grew bored and resentful, and they relapsed into their old habits. Most experts agree that if you take a more moderate and gradual approach, you're more likely to develop habits you can live with happily. Experts also recognize that the last word on healthful diet is not yet in. For years, salmon was condemned because of its high fat content. Next it was embraced because of its abundance of omega-3 fatty acids.

Then, in 1994, research discredited the purported benefits of omega-3 fatty acids. Similarly, in 1990, the cholesterol level of eggs was recalculated, and the American Heart Association raised its limit from three eggs a week to four. As time goes on, we can expect new realizations to prompt still other recommendations for changing our diets.

All these observations support the case for moderation. Yes, you can continue to have red meat. Choose a lean cut, such as flank steak, and broil it. Begin your meal with a soup or salad and accompany a 3-ounce portion with a steamed fresh vegetable and a potato or grain. By surrounding a small piece of meat with additional courses and side dishes, you are less likely to feel deprived. If you establish modest goals, such as cutting back on red meat to once a week, you will set yourself up for success.

As for chocolate cake, no one ever said you could never have another piece. First of all, don't think in terms of never. Just think in terms of today. And yes, you may splurge occasionally. Occasionally. As time goes on and you discover new delicacies, however, chances are you'll want to less and less.

Sex

Yes, you can and should make love if you want to. It cannot damage your heart, disturb your bypass, or hurt your incision. Are you afraid to have sex? Probably. Is your partner scared? Undoubtedly. Nearly everyone—patients and partners alike—worries about the ability to perform, about hurting the heart, about being too worried to enjoy the encounter, about how a scar alters sex appeal. Sometimes patients don't even realize they are worried, but somehow, mysteriously, they might discover they have lost their desire and their potency. If you used to have angina, which cried stop every time you approached orgasm, you probably have been conditioned by fear. Can worries like these ruin your experience? Maybe. But there are things you can do to protect it.

If you can, talk to your partner honestly and openly. Some people have trouble doing this. If you are one of them, communicate in whatever manner you communicate best, and remember that intercourse is only one facet of verbal and tactile communication that spells care, consideration, concern. Ideally, you and your partner have a tender, touching communication, which comforted you before surgery, in the ICU, and frequently since then. Even during your first week at home, there is no reason why kissing and caressing can't be a part of your time together watching television, listening to music, or talking in bed before you fall asleep. Sharing the worries which you and your partner are bound to have is part of this close communication. In bed, as in every other life arena, festering fear invites trouble. No one describes this as poignantly as Martha Weinman Lear in *Heartsounds*:

> It seemed crucial that he not know how scared I was. Lying there silently, as though my mind were on my pleasure. Watching him in the half-light that came from the bathroom, seeing the fingers pressed so slyly against his carotid artery, wondering what the pressure told him. Feeling his rhythm, the contact so sweet, and hearing him breathe heavily like that, and wondering if it was okay or too much. Then feeling his body go still. Was he all right? Did I dare ask?
>
> I felt poised at the edge of an irredeemable mistake. It would be dreadful to make him feel like an invalid here, of all places, impulse gone, confidence gone, good-bye, and maybe for good.
>
> And yet it might be even more dangerous to say nothing. For his body was in motion again now, and what if he was feeling pain, denying it, pushing himself to perform?
>
> "Do you want to rest for a moment?" I whispered.
>
> Wrong. He made a sound like a sob and fell away from me, and we lay silent, not touching in any way.

Surely, candid communication can help avert a disaster like this one. So can testing yourself. If you can walk up two flights of stairs without panting, feeling exhausted, or experiencing pain, you won't have heart trouble during sex. If you still feel apprehensive, consider masturbation. Pay attention to the way your heart pounds, your breathing speeds up, and your body feels hot. These are normal feelings.

Choose the time and place for your sexual encounters carefully. Make sure you are well rested and that you have time to rest afterward. Wait 2 to 3 hours after a heavy meal or alcoholic beverage. Adjust the thermostat in the room so the temperature is comfortable. Pick a moment when you and your partner are feeling good about yourselves and about each other; this is not the time to use sex to resolve an argument, dispel anxiety, or melt away hostility.

Don't rush. Be tender. Have fun. Light a candle. Play soft music. Engage in all your favorite foreplays and afterplays. If you like oral sex, by all means, indulge. If you enjoy caressing each other with baby oil, go right ahead. If you're nervous or worried, tell your partner and invite your partner to do likewise. Consider tempering anxiety with humor. Choose a comfortable position that does not strain your chest incision or hamper free breathing. Try lying on your side facing each other, or entering from behind. Men, try lying on your back with your partner on top; you will probably find the missionary position the most uncomfortable.

Despite good intentions, satisfactory sexual encounters may take some time. Surgery does lower the libido temporarily, as does anxiety. Be patient; be understanding. If impotence or lack of desire persists, discuss the problem with your doctor. Many cases of impotence are caused by medical problems that can be solved. Often these problems occur as side effects of medication, and altering your prescriptions may do the trick. Do not stop taking your medicine on your own, however. In addition, consult your physician if your heartbeat and breathing remain rapid for more than 20 minutes after orgasm, if you experience chest pain during

Don't rush. Be tender. Have fun.

intercourse, if you correlate insomnia with intercourse, or if you feel unusually tired the next day.

If difficulty with sex persists or if you find your doctor cannot help (some feel uncomfortable talking about sex), consider consulting a sex therapist. A few sessions may reveal the source of your difficulties and offer you specific suggestions for managing them.

One admonition: Having faced their mortality, many patients feel compelled to reevaluate their lives and, in this spirit, sometimes contemplate changing their sexual partners. If you are married or involved in a steady relationship, resist the urge. Affairs under these circumstances often promote guilt and anxiety, which put increased stress on the heart. The medical community makes the point with this stale joke:

Noticing a look of worry on his patient's face, the cardiologist asked, "What seems to be troubling you?"

The patient blushed and stammered, "Sex, doctor. Will I ever have sex again?"

"Of course," the cardiologist reassured him. "But only with your wife. We don't want you getting too excited."

Peer Support Groups

Peer support groups have been developed in many hospitals where heart surgery is performed. Usually, the best programs are those designed and supported by the professionals who take care of heart surgery patients. These peer support organizations hold monthly meetings, during which patients at various stages of recovery convene to share experiences, listen to speakers on various pertinent subjects, and make new friends. Some patients find these meetings reassuring and motivating. Others find them distasteful. Some patients come just a few times shortly after their surgery. Others become active for the long term, often volunteering their support to new patients. If your hospital has a support group, consider going. If nothing else, you will make contact with others who have walked your path, and they may be able to answer your questions. This peer group can be especially valuable if you have little questions you have not been able to discuss with your doctor.

If your hospital does not have a support group, look to the American Heart Association for a nearby chapter of Mended Hearts, the support group AHA has sponsored for 30 years. To locate Mended Hearts, call your local American Heart Association office or the national headquarters in Dallas at (214) 373-6300.

Paying Your Medical Bills

Medicare, Medicaid, and private medical insurance have turned paying hospital and physician bills into a nightmare. Filing for Medicare and Medicaid reimbursement is fraught with all the frustrating complexity typical of bureaucracy. And private medical insurance forms seem to be confusing by design. Third-party payers discovered long ago that the longer they can sustain a correspondence with their clients, the longer they can hold off paying a claim, and the more they can take advantage of their financial float. So pervasive is the resulting chaos that the *New England Journal of Medicine* published an article about it entitled "Health Care Rationing through Inconvenience: The Third Party's Secret Weapon" (August 31, 1989).

To make matters worse, medical bills, duplicate medical bills, and threatening letters begin piling up in your mailbox soon after you get home from the hospital, just when you're feeling vulnerable and overwhelmed by all the other problems associated with recovery. So many patients have been distraught by this mayhem that a new profession called medical claims assistance has emerged.

Free insurance counseling and assistance is available in every state through grants issued by the Medicare and Medicaid Assistance Program. At one time this program was managed nationally by the American Association of

Retired Persons (AARP), which trained volunteer counselors in the intricacies of filing Medicare and Medicaid forms. After training, the volunteers were tested and periodically updated to make sure that they kept pace with changing regulations. The volunteers helped organize your bills and file your claims, request an appeal when a claim was denied, and provide information to help analyze supplemental insurance policies. Since this program has been turned over to the states, it's hard to know exactly what services are available in each jurisdiction. For more information call your Area Agency on Aging.

Private medical claims assistants, most of whom gained their experience working for hospitals, physicians, their billing services, or insurance companies, will do the same and more for a fee. In addition to filing your claims for you, these professionals will also obtain missing records, track reimbursements, and ensure that you receive the maximum benefit from your insurance coverage. Some offer the added service of reviewing your insurance policies to make sure that you have adequate but not duplicate coverage.

If necessary, some will meet with you in your home to help you sort out your documents. Often, the service can be satisfactorily completed by mail, enabling you to work with professionals in a distant city. They charge either by the hour or by taking a percentage of your reimbursement. When these professionals are good, they can retrieve more from third party payers than you can on your own. Clients commonly recoup their fees and sometimes even come out ahead.

To obtain a referral, check with the office manager in your physician's office or the billing office at your hospital. If they cannot help you, call National Association of Professional Geriatric Care Managers, (602) 881-8008. We have also had good experience with Medical Claims Assistance Co., Inc. (800) 232-8090.

Since medical claims professionals are not licensed and there is no regulation governing their practice, you would be wise to get some personal recommendations before hiring someone. Ask the professional to whom you are referred for the names of some former clients you can speak to.

Managing Insistent Problems

While most patients experience satisfactory progress in the weeks following discharge, persistent complaints send a small proportion of patients back to their cardiologists earlier or more frequently than scheduled. Usually, physicians can solve the problem, but occasionally they shrug their shoulders and say, ''There's nothing wrong.'' Actually, they mean they can't find anything wrong. Put another way, they mean that if there were something seriously wrong, they would most likely spot it; since they don't see it, it is probably not a threatening problem, bothersome and worrisome though it might feel.

Like everything else, physicians prefer to be effective, and not being able to resolve their patients' medical complaints can make them uncomfortable. As a result, they may retreat. If you sense your physician is avoiding you, you may feel neglected, become angry, and perhaps depressed. If you find yourself with this problem, consider discussing it with a psychological counselor, who may be able to help you devise a strategy for solving it.

You might also consider asking your physician for a consultation with another cardiologist. In perplexing cases, a second opinion may provide valuable insight. At the very least, it can reassure you and your cardiologist that your treatment has been appropriate. Most doctors welcome the request for a second opinion, and you should not be embarrassed to ask for one.

Making Major Changes

Experts recommend making as few major changes in your life as possible for a year following surgery, and for good reason. Many patients have acknowledged that their surgery skewed their perspectives temporarily. Soon after surgery, they thought they wanted to retire or move to a new city or get married or get divorced. But a year or so later, they discovered they had made a mistake. In addition, when people move to a new city, leave their familiar workplace, or make a similarly major change, they often cut down their support systems just when they need them most. Finally, major life changes require people to strain their coping reserves; because of heart surgery, those coping reserves have already been strained. Overtaxing them might invite depression.

Returning to Work

You will probably get permission to return to work a month or so after surgery. Though you are returning to work, you will still get tired. Don't be surprised if you feel more tired than you have for weeks—just as you may have felt you had regressed when you left the ICU and then again when you left the hospital. Increased challenges are likely to exaggerate your vulnerability. Test your strength, make time to rest, save time to exercise, don't be impatient. Remember, many patients need a full year to overcome all the lingering effects of their surgery.

After bypass surgery, some patients elect to take a demotion, together with a pay cut, in order to reduce their stress. Most patients can return to their former employment. And many patients who had been disabled are suddenly well enough to work again. They return to jobs as mechanics, truck drivers, plumbers, and electricians, as well as to numerous office positions.

You will, of course, return to work with your doctor's approval, probably even a formal letter attesting to your well-being. Don't be surprised, however, if you experience discrimination at work. Some employers read "heart surgery" on an employment report and see the red flag of

Experts recommend making as few major changes in your life as possible for a year following surgery.

absenteeism and increased insurance costs. Others refuse newly returning workers any consideration or leeway whatsoever. Still others behave as though heart surgery is somehow catching and attempt to ostracize newly returning workers.

Sad to say, many patients have had unsavory experiences in this regard. A truck driver was told he had to resume all his responsibilities 4 weeks after surgery or lose his job. A counselor from Mended Hearts intervened on his behalf, and the patient was given a desk job temporarily. In a separate instance, a mechanic for a major airline was told to remain on leave until he was able to return full time and perform all his duties. Fortunately, this man's coworkers pitched in to help with his heaviest work until he could lift 60 pounds or more. A third patient, with a long and excellent record as a factory foreman, experienced serious discrimination when he moved to a new city and tried to get a job. Seven times he applied, and seven times, mysteriously, he got no job. On the eighth try, by coincidence, he encountered a different interviewer, who sent him to the company physician for a physical immediately.

"Usually you get your physical after you're hired. In my case, they changed the procedure, so I knew they were discriminating. But when the company Doc sent back a report that said I was in better shape than he was, they hired me," he reported.

Ideally, you'll have no such trouble. But if you do, you don't have to sit by and accept it. Perhaps your union or the social service department of your hospital can intervene on your behalf. If necessary, contact the American Civil Liberties Union, a private attorney, the federally funded legal services office nearest you, or a local office of the Equal Employment Opportunity Commission.

In addition, most experts—professionals as well as former patients—would advise against changing jobs at this time. There is the danger of potential discrimination as well as the added stress the change would create. If, when you return to work, you find yourself in a less desirable job because your old position was filled in your absence, don't quit precipitously. Consider your options carefully. If you must change jobs, you would do well to seek career counseling and get some good advice on how to handle your medical history when you apply for a new job.

Executive career counselor Diane Railton, president of Taylor Mark Stanley and Company, recommends withholding the information during the application and interview process as long as possible. If you are asked, you must answer truthfully because, she feels, there is nothing more damaging than lying. If no one asks, however, she advises that you say nothing until you are offered the job. At that point, say something like, "There's something in my medical history I feel I should tell you. I had bypass surgery 4 months ago, but I'm fine now. Of course, I'll give you a letter from my physician to confirm that, and I'll be happy to submit to whatever physical exam you require." Ms. Railton feels that the majority of employers she deals with would not reject a candidate on the basis of bypass.

Contact the social service department of your hospital or a career counselor for further guidance.

Points to Remember

❏ At first, stay alone for only a short time.

❏ Alternate activities and rest.

❏ Anticipate fatigue and increase exercise gradually.

❏ Begin massaging the chest incision during the third week.

❏ Continue breathing exercises through the fourth week.

❏ Try a bedtime ritual to cure insomnia.

❏ Approach a low-fat diet with a sense of adventure.

❏ Be patient and candid as you resume sex.

❏ Take advantage of peer support groups to share experiences and resolve concerns.

❏ Avoid making major changes for a year.

Chapter Eight

WHEN SOMEONE YOU LOVE HAS HEART SURGERY

As difficult as heart surgery can be, many patients contend that it is more difficult on the people who love them than on the patients themselves. Unwittingly, patients often reveal why.

Stresses Inherent in the Role of Supporter

Stuart McConnell reported, "The night before surgery, Helen cried and said she was worried I would die. 'I'm not going to die,' I said, 'but if I do, it doesn't matter because I'll be dead and I won't care.'"

Like many spouses and other primary supporters, Helen McConnell saw her husband's heart condition and his surgery as a threat to herself and her future, and she chastised herself for such selfish feelings. In the ensuing weeks, worry, guilt, and depression ate away at her.

Mr. McConnell entered the hospital the day before surgery, a scenario that is unusual today. That evening, while her husband managed his anxiety by asking the anesthesiologist, surgeon, respiratory therapist, physical therapist, and clinical nurse specialist a long list of questions, Mrs. McConnell went home to an empty house.

"I tried to read, but I couldn't concentrate. I turned on the television, but it hammered at my head. Finally, at midnight, I got into bed, but my heart was pounding and my mind was racing. I was whipped, but there was no sleep for me that night."

Meanwhile, Stuart McConnell took a sedative, which put him and his anxieties to rest.

Throughout her husband's hospitalization, Mrs. McConnell maintained her full-time job as a bookkeeper, did her husband's household chores as well as her own, and visited her husband after work every evening. She grew increasingly exhausted, felt her fears erupt every time his progress seemed to slow, and tried to marshal all her patience to cope with his periodic irritability. Once he got home, she felt responsible for his welfare. Afraid that he would overexert himself or suffer a setback, she hovered over him relentlessly. She reached to pour him a glass of juice and jumped up to get the door when the bell rang. She nagged at him to rest, and she nagged at him to exercise. As he exploded, "Get the hell off my back," she felt her anger and resentment boil.

"The primary supporters have a tremendous burden," asserted counselor Sally Kolitz. "They share all the patient's worries. Plus they have extra work. They get exhausted. They often experience verbal and emotional assault. But the system is not designed to give them support. Usually, that's reserved for the patient, but those who love him need it every bit as much."

The Value of Supporters

Few people are as vital to the patient's well-being as those who provide love and support. One patient, attesting to this truth, asserted that his dedication to his family was what sustained him through a precarious postoperative struggle. Although he was demoralized when wound infections and clots in his lungs kept him in the hospital for 3 weeks, he refused to surrender. "I won't give up," he insisted. "I can't chuck it because of my boys." Undoubtedly, this patient's commitment to his sons enhanced his will to rally, and when he was finally discharged, he anticipated an uncompromised recovery.

Many patients have attributed the speed and ease of their recuperation to good marriages, devoted children, and caring friends. Likewise, medical professionals observe that having someone to get well for often motivates patients to recover. These reports echo the results of a growing body of research that further ties meaningful social support to health and well-being. For example, in a study of 10,000 Israeli men at high risk for heart disease, those who believed they had good marriages developed angina at a surprisingly low rate. Similarly, a closely knit Pennsylvania population encountered unusually little heart disease, despite their high-fat diet, until the community-wide support system began to break apart. As its young people moved away, the incidence of disease increased.

People who enjoy a high level of social support have an easier time withstanding the impact of illness and the change it imposes on their lives. They benefit from the insights, information, and fresh ideas for solving problems that you, as supporters, can offer. You can also provide material aid, understanding, and distractions. As a result, you can help your loved ones gain a sense of control over the stressful events they are encountering, cope with the stress, view it more optimistically, and take care of themselves in the process.

According to our research, meaningful social support appears to play a specific role in reducing depression after heart surgery. When patients were given the first edition of this book before their operations, they often shared it with their spouses and children, who read it and used its contents to help the patients. Hospital personnel observed that these families appeared unusually free from distress, presumably because the book gave them whatever information they needed to assuage their concerns. Because the families were armed with information, they were in a good position to answer questions, offer reassurance, and solve problems creatively. The patients, we presume, took their cues from their families. They, too, seemed at ease, and they experienced depression at a surprisingly low rate. In other words, the patients benefited from the help their loved ones received.

Although we expected that patients without spouses would have surrogate supporters, our research revealed just the opposite: Those who had the benefit of support from a spouse tended to have the additional support of other family members as well. But where there was no spouse, there was a dearth of substitute support. Moreover, we discovered that where social support was lacking, there was a marked increase in depression. This finding jibes with other studies documenting that those who are unmarried or living alone are particularly prone to depression.

This finding arouses our concern for female patients. Since women develop heart disease an average of 10 years after men, and since women therefore go into bypass surgery at a more advanced age, they are more likely than men to be widowed by the time they need surgery. If, to compound the problem, these widows have not fully resolved their grief, they would be particularly vulnerable. Numerous studies have documented that grieving, lonely people are more prone to illness and death than their age peers. Research has also shown that people's coping reserves are finite, and if they have to cope with too many problems, they can deplete those reserves. Consequently, we worry that women who do not have spouses to support them may be at excessive risk for serious depression and other complications.

Even women who are married may face greater risk than married men. Although we do not have reliable data to document our suspicion, the experiences of the small number of women in our research suggest that the ways in which women give and receive support differ from those of men. Men, more than women, for example, feel uncomfortable in the role of nurturer, and we suspect that uneasy, tentative attempts at support may impede recovery in subtle but significant ways. Conversely, skillful and sensitive support can ease patients' crises tremendously, and those who provide it often find that their relationship with the patients they love grows stronger and more meaningful in the process.

Integral to being an effective supporter is taking care of yourself as well as the patient you love.

Acquiring Information

Just as patients benefit from information designed to help them cope with heart surgery, so you can benefit from knowledge as well. You might want to attend patient education classes and introductory sessions with the various therapists. At the same time, be sure to respect the patient's right, as well as your own, to have some private time with the medical personnel for confidential discussions. If you can strike a comfortable balance between protecting individual privacy and participating constructively in the presurgical consultations, you can set the scene for mutual respect and understanding.

In addition to learning about surgery and recovery, it's a good idea to get the following information for yourself:

Where can I wait during surgery?

What kind of progress reports can I expect and how long will I have to wait for the first one? (Some hospitals are wonderfully considerate of the anxiety families feel from the moment they kiss their loved one good luck. And while these hospitals are good about providing progress reports, the first one often comes when the heart–lung machine takes over the patient's cardiac and respiratory functions, sometimes as long as 2 hours into surgery.)

Who will deliver these reports?

When can I speak to the doctor?

When can I first see the patient following surgery, and what will he or she look like? What kinds of tubes, catheters, wires, and machinery can I expect to encounter?

Will the patient be sleeping or awake? Coherent or foggy? Will his complexion look healthy or wan? Will I see blood? (The answers to these questions depend, in part, on how soon after surgery visitors are allowed into the ICU.)

What are the visiting hours in the ICU?

If I feel concerned between visiting hours, whom can I call?

Keep pencil and paper handy to note questions, jot down key points, and list additional questions. Answers to the first questions always provoke new ones, and in the stress of the moment, unless you write them down, you may forget them.

After the patient-orientation session, many supporters and patients find it helpful to review together what they learned and questions they still have. Sometimes supporters and patients interpret information differently and remember different points. Going over the information clarifies the truth and creates an opportunity to share feelings. Honest talk can clear the air and bring people closer together, provided each person respects the other's coping preferences and need for privacy.

Conflicting Coping Styles

One husband who attended all his wife's surgical education sessions found the experience upsetting. Though the patient eagerly sought every possible detail, her husband found that each new bit of knowledge made him worry more. He would have done better to wait outside.

Another supporter encountered difficulty when she sensed her husband didn't share her need to talk about his forthcoming surgery. "I had a very tough time before my husband's surgery. My husband is very independent. He had to go into the hospital himself, get all his information himself, and when I came to visit him, he insisted on talking about anything but his operation. It was so frustrating for me, I left his room in tears.''

To cope with impending surgery, this patient had to demonstrate to himself that he was invincible. He always handled problems in his life alone, and this one would be no exception. His wife needed to talk through her fears, but she realized that it would be wrong to impose her anxieties on her husband. Fortunately, she encountered the patient education specialist, who lent her an untiring ear. This sensitive nurse listened to all her fears, answered all her questions, and promised to see her in the surgical waiting room.

If your coping style differs from the patient's, you must defer to his. But you must meet your own needs as well. If you need to talk, find someone else to talk to. By taking care of yourself, you will improve your capacity to be a good supporter later.

Empathy

Tuning in to the kind of support that is genuinely helpful to another person—a child, a lover, a friend, a patient—means being a compassionate listener. It involves the skills psychologists include when they talk about empathy or active listening. For patients coping with heart surgery, this is the most important service any loved one can provide.

When you listen compassionately, you experience another person's feelings as if they were your own. You make no judgments about what the other person is feeling. You simply try to understand it. In so doing, you acknowledge that you respect the other person. At the same time, you refrain from implying that any emotional response is better or worse than any other.

As Sylvia Turner kissed her husband goodnight the evening before his surgery, he addressed the emotions that held his body rigid. "I'm so terrified of tomorrow," he whispered. "I'm afraid I'll never kiss you good night again."

"Of course you're terrified," Sylvia Turner replied. "Anyone going into heart surgery could be frightened. But remember that the doctor said you're an excellent candidate. It's OK to be scared, but you will do fine. You're going to come through this operation like a champ."

Sylvia Turner accepted her husband's apprehension and acknowledged its legitimacy. She also reminded him that, while his fears were understandable, there were many reasons to be optimistic. That's very different from saying his fears were wrong.

Too many spouses, themselves feeling threatened by the experience or the emotions it evokes, might respond, "Don't worry. Everything will be all right." That's what Anita Brown did.

Never, to Anita Brown's recollection, had her husband faltered in his strength. He had built a brilliant business, and he had made all financial and practical decisions for his family. Now 76 and retired, he continued to portray confidence and independence, and Anita Brown admitted that, after 52 years of marriage, she leaned on her husband shamelessly. Imagine the scene when, on the fourth day after Gerald Brown's surgery, Anita Brown walked into her husband's room and found him sobbing like a little boy.

"He was terrified that he had lost his mind, and I was terrified that I was losing him," Anita Brown remembered. "You know, before the operation he said everything would be fine, and I believed him. I was worried, sure, but I never really believed he would die. When I saw him in the intensive care unit, he didn't look so good, but I knew it was temporary. But when I saw him crying, that was too much. He shouldn't know I'm upset, I thought, so I said, 'Gerry, don't cry. You're gonna be fine. There's nothing to worry about. Remember, Joey's coming from California to see you tonight.' "

Anita Brown hoped that her platitudes would dry her husband's tears and bring the smile of self-confidence back into his eyes. Perhaps making these statements helped her deny that her husband was not the emotional Samson she wished him to be. But they did not resolve Gerald Brown's own fears about his physical and emotional weakness, nor did they erase the feelings that caused his tears in the first place. By offering banalities and implying that she did not understand what he was feeling, Anita Brown alienated herself from her husband. She might have helped her husband while strengthening the bond between them if she had empathized with his misery.

"It's OK to cry," she might have said. "There's nothing wrong with crying when you're fed up with being sick. I understand your frustration, and maybe crying will help a little."

In the day or so before surgery, empathy can take the form of acknowledging fear or respecting denial. In the days, weeks, and months afterward, it can shift to understanding anxiety, fear, and anger. Empathy can open the door to solving real problems:

I appreciate your frustration at not being able to talk to the doctor. Perhaps we can ask him to allow 10 extra minutes tomorrow?

Of course you're entitled to feel blue. Listening to Bill Cosby always used to perk you up. What do you think about getting a Cosby tape from the library?

I would be short-tempered, too, if I got tired just from reading the morning newspaper. But we need to find a way not to take out our frustrations on each other.

Empathy suggests, "She really does understand," and while understanding doesn't eradicate the problem, it's a good beginning.

Whether patients acknowledge fear going into surgery or not, most are affected by it at least on an unconscious level. While candor is important, destroying a person's defenses can be devastating, and a supporter who tries to drag an admission of fear from a patient who seems at peace can wreck the patient's self-protective mechanisms. As the moments before surgery draw closer, take your cues from your loved one. And as you kiss him good luck, you would do well to imply that survival and recovery are certain. A statement like "I'll see when you wake up" can do wonders to lower anxiety.

Coping with the ICU

You usually can visit the ICU briefly within an hour or so after surgery. It takes this long for patients to be settled and hooked up to their various machines and monitors. When you see your loved one for the first time, he will probably still be anesthetized and lying utterly still. He may have surprisingly good color. He is likely to be covered up to his chin, so you won't see the myriad tubes and catheters that have been plugged into his body. What you will see is the endotracheal tube, which is taped to the face and connected to the respirator, and the nasogastric tube, which emerges from the nose and is also taped in place.

"When the counselor invited me into the ICU for the first time, I felt bombarded by mixed emotions," the husband of a bypass patient recalled. "I was relieved, of course, because the counselor assured me my wife was OK. But I felt really skittish about seeing her in that condition. Everything I had heard about the ICU spooked me, and I followed that counselor in dread."

This is a common moment for tears.

"It's relief," assessed Barbara Friedman. "They've spent all this energy worrying. And they're exhausted. Once they see with their own eyes that everything is as it should be, they let go. After a quick peek to reassure themselves, I urge our patients' families to go home, have a cup of tea, and get some rest."

Being Supportive in the ICU

In retrospect, former patients feel a number of items would have made their time in the ICU easier. Before visiting in the ICU, you might put together a help package based on these suggestions. If your patient wears glasses, bring an extra pair in case the pair he was wearing before surgery didn't find its way to the ICU. To help an intubated patient communicate, bring a large clipboard with plenty of big sheets of paper and a short, fat pencil. These are the easiest implements to use for a patient whose arm is strapped to an IV board. Since nurses step away from the bedside momentarily, bring something an intubated patient can use to attract attention. A large paper fastener or a hemostat—a medical instrument that looks like a cross between eyebrow tweezers and a pair of scissors—is ideal because you can clip it to the bed sheet and the patient can bang it against the bed rail. Sometimes patients also appreciate having a clock and a Walkman-type radio. Before bringing in these last two items, however, you would be wise to look over the ICU setup, assess the appropriateness of the idea, and mention it to the nurses. Often patients are in the ICU so briefly and the quarters are so cramped that bringing in this kind of equipment would create more problems than it would solve.

If you are visiting when your patient rouses from anesthesia, you can contribute significantly to reorienting him. Since general anesthesia always disorients patients, they benefit tremendously from hearing, "You're fine, Dad. Your surgery is over and everything is OK." Telling him what day and time it is also helps. Patients characteristically drift into and out of awareness for several hours and often need these messages repeated.

Though visits in the ICU are short, you can fulfill a vital role during this difficult period. While your patient is intubated, help him communicate nonverbally by calmly and quietly attempting to understand his message. In the event of difficulty, do not ask him questions he cannot answer. Talk calmly and quietly. Reassure him that you will figure out what he wants even if it takes some time. Pat his arms. Soothe him verbally. Devise a progression of yes–no questions that he can answer by moving his head or blinking his eyes.

Encourage him to lie quietly and permit the medical staff to take care of him. Encourage him to trust the medical personnel.

If he remains disoriented after the intubation tube is removed and if he is aware he is not himself, urge him to talk about his fears. Pat his head, stroke his forehead, caress his cheek; touching provides additional reassurance.

You can also help by reaffirming that he is entitled not to like the medical treatments that are imposed on him and that he would be justified in feeling angry at the nurses and therapists whose treatments feel like torture. If you say something like, "Of course you feel irritable when you hurt"; or "You don't have to like your treatments; you just have to take them," you will validate his anger and help him to realize that the nurses understand it and don't take it personally. Tufts University Professor of Psychiatry Richard Blacher discovered that when patients believed that their anger will not alienate their caregivers, they are less likely to encounter serious emotional distress.

Above all, in the unlikely event that your patient makes irrational claims, do not argue with him or attempt to convince him that his perceptions are wrong.

One patient in the ICU was terribly agitated because he was convinced something was wrong with his IV. Before long, the patient's growing distress had drawn two nurses and a physician's assistant to his bedside. Foolishly, these three professionals argued louder and louder that his IV was fine.

At that moment, the patient's daughter came to the bedside and took over management of the problem.

"Dad, I think there's something wrong with your IV, but I can't figure out what it is. Will you please help me and I'll see that it's fixed," she said.

In the stupor of his medications, the patient didn't convey his ideas too clearly, but with patience and persistence, the daughter was able to discern that he was distressed because the IV tube was twisted and he was afraid the fluids could not flow freely.

"Do you think it would help if we shortened the IV tube so that it couldn't twist?" she asked.

He heaved a thankful yes. The nurse took a link out of the IV tubing, and the patient relaxed.

When patients respond irrationally, do not try to convince them they are wrong. First, it doesn't work, and second, since their disorientation is temporary, it doesn't matter. What does matter is that their anxiety is put to rest. That can be accomplished by assuming the problem, as they perceive it, is valid and by attempting to solve it.

Being Supportive for the Duration of Recovery

Once your patient moves into step-down care and throughout the recuperative period at home, your role changes. Now, rather than soothing and calming him, you must direct your energies to reinforcing the self-help messages of the medical personnel.

"I know it hurts to cough, but you have to do it. I know you're tried, but you have to walk" is the theme.

You can also help by restoring the patient's sense of control as much as possible and by attempting to make him feel whole, needed, and important. Ask your patient for his opinion, seek his advice, and offer him choices. Permit him his anger and fears, and share yours. Resist the inclination to protect him from problems.

Anxiety and Its Consequences

Too often, the supporters' worries get in their way. Feeling threatened, they often make inappropriately optimistic remarks. When they cannot acknowledge their fears and those of the patient they love, they sometimes erect a wall of isolation. And when patients sense that their families cannot handle their illness, they feel abandoned.

One supporter, terrified that her husband would never work again, could not face his anxieties over the same thought. A construction foreman whose angina had kept him from work for 6 months, he was obsessed about what kind of job he could hold after his recovery. His wife was aware of his concerns, but she could not bear to discuss them. Whenever possible, she changed the subject. When pressed, she ignored its significance.

"What are you thinking about that now for? You're still in the hospital. Worry about getting home first," she advised, wedging an uncomfortable distance between them.

Another wife, afraid to agitate her husband, stopped consulting him as problems arose concerning the country home they were building. Whereas before surgery they talked to the contractor together, after his surgery she shielded him from such talks. While he was in the hospital, she lied that she hadn't been in touch with the contractor. After he came home, she pretended someone else called on the phone.

"One time, the contractor called to say the plumbing fixtures hadn't been delivered. Another time, he said he had to put the electrician on another job for a week. Delays like this drive my husband crazy, and I know stress is bad for him," Patricia Teller explained.

While Mrs. Teller meant well, she angered her husband and strained their relationship. She worried silently about distressing him, and he quietly seethed that he was not as vulnerable as she presumed. Instead of sharing their feelings about his health and their retirement home, each tried to cope separately. They stopped relating, and they stopped communicating.

To be sure, Mrs. Teller's behavior was prompted by concern for Robert Teller's welfare. At home, separated from constant medical supervision, she feared stress would trigger a setback. She was unclear about exactly what activities or emotional involvements constituted stress, so she attempted to prevent them all.

Mrs. Teller's errors are common. Many supporters are uncertain about how their patients should be feeling from day to day, and exactly what activities and involvements are safe. Out of fear and uncertainty, they smother their patients, and the patients become less independent and more sedentary than they had been in the hospital. When patients have a bad day, as they all do, their supporters hover even more closely. To break the cycle, patients often hide their discomforts, thus increasing the distance between the parties.

In truth, Mr. Teller was more frustrated by his wife's overprotection than he would have been by the construction delays. If he had been informed, he would have felt a sense of participation, and that feeling would have tempered his frustrations.

Of course, everyone is different, and sometimes patients find an element of comfort in overprotection.

"I was grateful for my wife's vigilance," said one such patient. "I liked knowing she was concerned. She was there all the time, watching me. She'd wake up in the middle of the night to make sure I was breathing, and I knew that if anything happened, she'd see that I got help."

In most instances, however, patients find that hovering supporters emphasize unpleasant feelings of insecurity and unworthiness. If patients already view themselves as damaged goods and worry that others view them similarly, reminders of their fragility can infuriate them. Their anger can then alienate family and friends, and a bad situation gets worse.

One former patient recalled the frustration he felt as almost everyone he knew made a special effort to take care of him. "It was as though I was living in a padded world. Even months after my surgery, when the doctor had given me the green light to do everything, my secretary jumped up to take my briefcase when I came in to work in the morning. My tennis partner didn't hit as close to the lines as he used to. My buddies wouldn't even get into a good debate over politics anymore. Everybody treated me as though they were afraid I would break, and I hated it."

If overprotection is a problem, the solution is probably increased knowledge. When you and your loved one are confident that recovery is progressing properly, when you are convinced that certain activities and involvements are therapeutic, and when you feel you can distinguish between signs of trouble and benign symptoms, you will probably be able to relax. Therefore, you need to keep asking questions until you have concrete and satisfactory answers. Knowing vaguely that a patient should "do a little more but continue taking it easy" isn't good enough. How far should he be walking this week? How many hours can she work? Which responsibilities can she assume? In what way is healing pain different from heart pain? When you get satisfying answers to questions like these, you will probably be able to provide constructive support to your patient. As the two of you share your concerns and reassure each other, you're likely to strengthen the bond between you.

Feeling Overwhelmed

The stresses that you experience during this period can wear you down. Often, supporters let their hectic schedules, their worries, and their dedication drive them to exhaustion. As one wife admitted, "While my husband was in the hospital, I ran on nervous energy. I was at the hospital before eight every morning to help him with breakfast, and I stayed until after dinner because he was too weak to feed himself. By the time he came home, I was a little run down.''

Another supporter agreed. ''The driving back and forth was hard. Anxiety made it worse. And once I got home at night, the incessant phone calls drove me to distraction. People meant well, but I couldn't deal with it anymore. In desperation, I put a nightly progress report on my answering machine and turned the ringer off.''

Whether the supporters are men or women, they are invariably faced with new challenges which, in light of the surrounding stresses, become more difficult than they would otherwise be. When their husbands are hospitalized, some older women confront their first experiences with bank accounts and insurance policies. Old or young, wives sometimes feel uncomfortable coming home alone late at night or dealing with mechanical emergencies in the house. When the patients are women, many men experience the alien role of nurturer. Some have no idea how to do the laundry, feel helpless in the kitchen or the supermarket, and quake at the prospect of being responsible for their wives' welfare.

''We had been married 40 years, but when my wife came home from the hospital, I didn't know what to say to her or what to do for her. My hands would shake if I had to give her medicine,'' one husband admitted.

Unmarried patients present other difficulties for supporters. Often children or siblings must leave their families and travel to another city to care for a recuperating patient. Divided loyalties and conflicting responsibilities invariably add to their concerns.

Even when someone feels comfortable as a primary supporter, heart surgery can exaggerate the inherent difficulties in the role. A wife admitted, ''Between worrying about my job, his well-being, and my crazy schedule, I got lost in the woods of worry. I couldn't figure out which ones were important and which were trivial. I needed help sorting out what to focus on and what to forget.''

Often, supporters let their hectic schedules, their worries, and their dedication drive them to exhaustion.

Guilt and Resentment

Sometimes feelings of guilt and responsibility surface. One wife, whose husband was taking iron tablets to cure his postoperative anemia, served liver his first night home because she knew it was rich in iron.

"After dinner, he got pain in his chest and needed nitroglycerine, and I was sure I had caused the problem," she recalled.

When patients understand the strains their supporters feel, the patients can do a lot to ease them. Sometimes, however, patients are so preoccupied with their own problems that they become oblivious to anyone else's. One former patient, proud of the superwoman who was his wife, breezily dismissed questions about her difficulties by saying, "She rose to the occasion."

In addition, patients' irritability, a common sequel to surgery, eats away at their supporters' capacity to cope. In the weeks following surgery, some patients become demanding and difficult to please. Supporters occasionally find themselves turning their own lives inside out to care for someone whose personality they hardly recognize. The slower the patient's recovery and the lower the levels of empathy and communication, the more intense these problems become.

One patient, seriously depressed but unwilling to face his depression, turned away from his family entirely. Months after his surgery, he seemed a different person. Whereas he had always been involved with his family and their activities, he suddenly disappeared for days at a time. When he was home, he was sullen and remote. Understandably, his wife was devastated.

"I had worked so hard to be supportive and take care of him," she complained. "He never acknowledged the toll his illness took on me. And then he just shut me out. Always before we talked through dinner and long into the night. And now we don't talk at all."

This example represents the extreme. More often the changes are less dramatic.

"There were no big issues, but the little issues never quit," one wife commented. "He wanted a turkey sandwich for lunch, and as soon as I made it, he asked for tuna. I tried so hard to please him, but it seemed I couldn't do anything right."

Typically, patients vent their anger at their supporters, the people they care about most. Unconsciously, they realize that these people, whose love they can rely on, make safe targets. While the anger is, in a perverse fashion, a statement of trust, it is not easy to take. The supporters, who have dedicated themselves to caregiving, lose their patience under the barrage of irritability. Supporters also feel guilty because of their resentment and to some degree because they are healthy. Paradoxically, while supporters initially feel overwhelmed by too many concerns, after the patient is home for a short time, their focus grows uncomfortably narrow.

"Before I realized it, I had no life of my own. I was with my husband constantly. I served him. I walked with him. I tried new recipes for him. I drove him to cardiac rehab. In the process, I stopped my volunteer work. I never had lunch with my friends. I never thought about anything unrelated to heart disease," one supporter said.

Another supporter agreed. "I'm so tired of thinking about illness. My husband is so self-centered. He's preoccupied with his food and his rest and his exercise. He says he needs to be in order to get well and stay well. But he won't give up demanding the attention that goes with being sick."

As if these problems weren't enough, they become aggravated when, in a well-intentioned attempt to support the patient, friends and extended family overlook the supporters' own need for help.

Resolving the Problems

Fortunately, these difficulties usually resolve themselves within a few months after surgery. As patients grow stronger and healthier, their anger and depression abate. They resume their old life-style or adjust to a new one; they lose their preoccupation with themselves; and their former personalities reemerge. During the crisis, however, you need to protect yourself.

Self-protection begins when you relinquish feelings of responsibility for your loved one's recovery. If your patient does not recuperate quickly or refuses to take responsibility for his recovery, don't get trapped into feeling you have failed. You did not make your loved one sick, and you cannot fix his troubles. Ultimately, the responsibility for doing the work of recovery lies with the patient.

In addition to freeing yourself from this impossible responsibility, you must make sure that you take care of yourself. Many people who have traveled this road recommend asking for help. Friends, neighbors, and relatives appreciate feeling needed and often welcome specific requests. "Please cook dinner tonight. Please take the clothes to the cleaners or stop at the supermarket or stay with Fred on Friday afternoon."

Communicate your feelings with your patient and solicit his support for you. One wife's experience dramatizes how effective this approach can be. Although her husband was recuperating well, she found herself growing increasingly exhausted and resentful. As she walked in from work one night, she burst into tears.

"Honey, what's wrong?" her startled husband asked.

"I'm so tired of going to work and taking care of this house and taking care of you. I know it's not your fault that you got sick, but I can't help the way I feel," she cried.

"What can I do to help you?" her husband asked.

After thinking a minute, she responded, "If you'd just do the breakfast dishes so I didn't have to walk into a dirty kitchen when I come home from work, I think it would help."

The next morning, her husband not only did the dishes, but scrubbed the counters, shined the stove top, and polished the refrigerator. He was delighted to be doing something that mattered. When his wife came home that evening, she felt a rush of appreciation and partnership instead of the familiar resentment. By telling her husband what she needed, she, as well as her husband, got more than just a clean kitchen.

If giving health care seems overwhelming, call the Visiting Nurse Association or the American Heart Association for supportive health services. If finances perplex you, ask an officer at the bank to help demystify Certificates of Deposit and checkbooks; she is paid to offer such assistance. If you can afford to, hire a maid for a few hours a week or take the laundry to a wash and fold. If money is too tight, perhaps you can get some volunteer help from your local church or synagogue. Alternatively, you might trade favors with a friend.

Most important, set aside time for yourself. This is not time taken away from the patient; it is time to replenish your own resources so that you can be a better caregiver. Unburden yourself by confiding in an empathetic friend. Talk to others who have been in your position, and get reassurance that this difficult period will end. Make arrangements to attend the regular meeting of your professional association or go out to lunch with a friend or keep important appointments or take a bubble bath. Invariably, professionals agree, if you can compensate for your stresses and restore facets of your normal life, you will speed the crisis of illness to an end. If you cannot reduce your stress with efforts like these, seek crisis intervention counseling for yourself. A professional can probably view your problems with enough perspective to help you devise effective solutions.

Ultimately, the crisis will be over. Rarely is it resolved leaving the participants the same as they had been before.

"The experience is too profound for people to walk away from it untouched," believes Miami psychologist

Sally Kolitz. "One way or another, patients and their supporters are bound to be different afterwards."

Occasionally, as patients grow stronger and reclaim their former roles, their supporters have trouble because they feel they are no longer needed. Conversely, recuperating patients may feel reluctant to relinquish the sick role even though, by all medical measures, they should be functioning as well people. Difficulties like these as well as less clear-cut problems, especially among couples whose marriages were shaky before the surgery, sometimes result in permanently impaired relationships. At least as frequently, however, families and friendships emerge stronger and closer for having come through the crisis together.

On a practical level, supporters discover they have capabilities they never would have imagined possible. One wife realized how vulnerable she had been because she had always relied on her husband to take care of problems with the plumbing and the roof. After her husband's recuperation, she took an adult ed course in basic home maintenance and acquired sufficient knowledge to speak with authority when she interacted with repair people. Whether supporters take on new roles permanently or resort to old ones, many emerge from the experience feeling more independent and self-reliant. Others discover the powerful bonding crises can promote.

"When my father had bypass, I came from New York and my sister came from Denver, and for the first time in years we had something more important to say to each other than, 'What's new?' " one adult child observed. "Our whole family is closer as a result."

Similarly, many marriages have benefited. Partners commonly claim the experience made them appreciate each other more, understand each other better, and place new value on the times they shared.

One former patient summed up the impact of the crisis this way: "It's so easy to take a marriage for granted. When my husband realized that I could die and I realized how much I needed him, we were shaken out of our complacency. Life and love are so fragile. Now we devote a lot of time to protecting them.''

Points to Remember

❏ Satisfy your own needs to acquire information and resolve concerns.

❏ Try to listen to your patient and accept his feelings without being judgmental.

❏ Be reassuring and comforting in the ICU.

❏ Encourage independence later.

❏ Avoid being overprotective.

❏ Take care of yourself.

❏ Seek help and social support when you need it.

❏ Try to restore facets of your normal life as quickly as possible.

Chapter Nine

MORE ABOUT DEPRESSION

To a great extent, depression after heart surgery is a normal response. The antithesis to the stress and anxiety of the immediate pre- and postoperative periods, it is the mind's retreat, a hideaway for repair and restoration.

As the preceding chapters revealed, depression occasionally descends while patients are in the ICU, but it usually waits until after they test their strength in a regular hospital room. This is when they discover how weak they are and begin to question the effectiveness of their surgery. In their weakened condition, they tend to perceive small difficulties as major problems. As they struggle, their families tend to coddle them, and they feel worse. Going home sets patients up for a recurrence of these feelings. Most patients ready for discharge have overcome the fatigue they felt when they were first moved to a regular hospital room, and by the time they are discharged, they feel fine. Then the trip home exhausts them, and the pattern repeats. To aggravate it, the limits of recuperation seem more exaggerated at home than they did in the protective environment of the hospital, and patients sometimes conclude the road to recovery is more tortuous than they had thought. Normal reactive depression results. It can come and go for as long as 3 months. Usually, the bad days grow more distant from one another, and then they disappear.

Reactive Depression and Grief

The depression that patients normally experience after surgery strongly resembles the grief that survivors, particularly spouses, feel when a loved one dies. Peggy Eastman, contributing editor for *Self* magazine, described her feelings of despair after her husband had been killed in an airplane crash. Her appetite disappeared. Sleep became an elusive friend to be lured, but only briefly, by sedatives. Panic, like a stalking cat, caught her off guard. It attacked unprovoked with startling surprise, and smothered perspective and reason before succumbing to a Xanax (Upjohn [alprazolam]) pill. Worse, it made her feel ''freakish, distanced, set apart. . . . I was a pariah, as if I had done something embarrassing, something that made people around me feel uncomfortable. What people seemed to want was for me to be 'recovered,' returned as quickly as possible to the person they knew before. But I couldn't do it.''

Like grief, the depression that follows surgery has a specific reason. Like grief, it is painful but usually not dangerous. It mimics clinical depression, which is a chronic illness that often demands active and prolonged medical treatment. But unlike more menacing depressions, it is usually self-limiting. Within several months it should go away. In addition—and this is important—normal reactive depression rarely causes long-term feelings of worthlessness and guilt.

The Many Faces of Depression

For all this seemingly clear-cut description, reactive depression can present a muddy multitude of portraits, some diametrically different from others. While some of the pictures are benign, others are pernicious. And the line between them, characterized largely by the severity and duration of symptoms, is easily blurred. Because the signs can be so ambiguous, lingering depression can go undiagnosed and untreated. Yet in its most severe forms it can impose such heavy feelings of hopelessness that victims contemplate suicide. This is rare; however, since reactive depression does, on occasion, become dangerously severe, we will try to resolve the ambiguity.

In its most benign form, depression seems no different from the transient pessimism and disinterest most people experience briefly when the weather turns gloomy or work gets boring. While it feels heavy, the weight is not unbearable and it lifts readily. In its more debilitating forms, depression can make independent adults regress into a dependent, childlike state. It can make people who, by all medical measures, should feel strong and healthy feel sick and weak, sometimes for years on end. "It was the darkest, most terrifying and painful period of my life," said one patient who first encountered depression following his coronary bypass surgery. "It was more frightening than being in the Normandy Invasion, more painful than losing my wife, and worse than any other illness I've ever had."

Like people suffering from less serious forms, those who experience worrisome depression usually, but not always, feel sad, discouraged, or hopeless. In addition, they often lose interest in activities which ordinarily stimulate them and find that nothing brings them pleasure. They may lose their drive and their persistence, saying they just don't care. While depression is almost always associated with some of these feelings, some victims withdraw rather than complain. Refusing to see family and friends, they may spend hours lying listlessly in bed or sitting in a darkened room. Sometimes, depression, especially after surgery, is marked solely by feeling physically sick.

Those who are depressed often complain that they cannot concentrate. Sometimes their thinking slows down; their memory fails, and they find themselves easily distracted. Yet they often brood and become obsessed about their physical health. They may become phobic or suddenly panic. Frequently they look gloomy and feel anxious. They may cry for no apparent reason. Pernicious depression often makes people suffer low self-esteem. Ridden by a sense of guilt and worthlessness, they often feel responsible for events beyond their control. At worst, they may hallucinate, become obsessed about some presumed sinfulness or worthlessness, or worry that they will succumb to illness, poverty, or some vague source of destruction. With these feelings may come a fear of dying, thoughts of suicide, or death wishes.

"Everyone would be better off I were dead" is a frequent lament.

In addition, victims of depression may experience a change in eating habits. Many patients lose their appetite, but some begin to eat compulsively. In either event, weight changes can be significant. Depressed people may sleep excessively, or they may have trouble sleeping. While some can't fall asleep, some others wake repeatedly during the night. Most frequently, patients find themselves awake for the day at 4 or 5 in the morning.

When people are depressed, they invariably feel enervated even though they have exerted no physical effort. They may move more slowly than usual and find a task as simple as writing a check too difficult to tackle. Yet, in depression, some people encounter uncontrollable restlessness. They may fidget, pace the floor, wring their hands, pull at their skin or hair. They may burst out shouting, complaining, or expostulating. Conversely, they may become much less verbal than usual, punctuating their infrequent speech with long pauses. Their speech may become slow, droning, monotonal.

The possible profiles of depression are so varied that three depressed people might bear no resemblance to each other. Hal Lear, the urologist whose heart surgery is chronicled in *Heartsounds,* portrays the classic picture of depression, together with the confusing frustration it imposes on family and loved ones. Martha Weinman Lear writes:

> Wearing the same clothes day after day, and surely no accident that they were the dullest-colored things in his closet. Lying on the bed, near-motionless for hours on end, fully dressed, staring at nothing, fiddling mindlessly with the middle button of his shirt, the one over the center of his scar; buttoning and unbuttoning, buttoning and unbuttoning.
>
> I began to grow impatient with him myself. Shave for heaven's sake. Comb your hair. There are worse things in life than a bad memory. . . .

Refusing to see family and friends, they may spend hours lying listlessly in bed or sitting in a darkened room.

Once I said it aloud. We sat at the table, he poking at his food, and he was trying to say something but the simple word he wanted was not there; he struggled for it and grimaced and banged his head with his fist, crying out, "What has happened to my mind?" and I said, "Oh come on, stop doing that number. It's no tragedy if you can't think of a word."

He looked at me not with anger, which would have been tolerable, but with the deepest sadness. It hurt my eyes. I felt ashamed.

He is going down the tube, and I don't want to go with him [she told a friend]. But I love him. What in God's name do I mean? I didn't understand myself at all.

Like Martha Weinman Lear, who was distraught by her husband's depression, the wife of another patient found herself a helpless bystander during her husband's recovery. Thomas Darling had always felt in charge of his life. After surgery, he felt he had lost control but denied he was depressed. He projected blame for his condition on his wife and made a series of inappropriate, flailing attempts to regain control. As the following letter written by his wife reveals, his depression was hard to recognize.

Within several months of the open-heart surgery, there was a marked change in my husband's personality. Where before he was close with his children and with me, he became distant, not having much to say. He would take a day off from work and go for a ride alone, which is completely out of character. The family was most patient with him thinking he was just temporarily depressed. . . . He moved out of our home saying he was staying with "friends" (unnamed) because he needed to be alone for a while. . . . Contact with old friends was kept to a minimum and his former great sense of humor was absent. . . . By mid-January he announced that he was marrying a former acquaintance of ours but soon he was again contacting me by phone and we met several times for dinner or a drink. . . . He will now say that he is unhappy and does not know what he wants in life other than to be happy for his few remaining years. His subsequent physicals have been very good except for a slight extra heartbeat for which he takes

medication. . . . He went to the Pritikin Longevity Center in California for two weeks in the hope of finding a correct diet, exercise,
and kicking the smoking habit. He was successful but has gone
back to his old habits. At this point I feel that he definitely does
love me and his family, that he is caught up in an affair he wants
out of, but I do not know how to help him.

In the cloak of depression, Hilda Tower looks different
still. Although her cardiologist claimed her surgery a success, two months afterward, she was still having chest pain
and some shortness of breath. Her whole body felt out of
sync. Though she was always tired, she could not sleep.
She went to bed at 10 only to wake again at 11 feeling
nervous—so nervous she couldn't stay in bed, so nervous
she wanted to bury her head in her pillow and scream. Although she had been back to work for 2 weeks, she could
not concentrate.

"One day, while I was doing some paperwork, I got
nervous for no reason at all," she remembered. "If I hadn't
been in an embarrassing situation, I could have cried just
as easily as not."

The Elusiveness of Depression

When the same syndrome can look so different in three
people, it's no wonder that health professionals sometimes
miss diagnosing it. Yet studies estimate that as many as
32% of all medical patients suffer from serious depression
and that up to half of them go unidentified.

The problem is compounded by ambiguity in the term
depression. Since medical professionals sometimes use the
word to denote transient sadness, pessimism, or disinterest,
the observation that a patient is depressed does not always
prompt serious concern. This problem is further confounded
when symptoms of depression mirror problems that ordinarily accompany a given medical condition. For example,
all patients tire easily after heart surgery. Some report they

don't feel like themselves for a year. In addition, heart surgery patients commonly complain they have no appetite and cannot concentrate. When Albert Peterson complained 2 months after his operation that he felt listless, his memory was failing, and he couldn't enjoy his favorite foods, was he dangerously depressed or experiencing normal recovery?

Medical professionals sometimes disregard depression because they assume it is consistent with and appropriate to illness, surgery, and recovery. If depression is defined as transient discouragement, this assumption is valid. Certainly, anyone who experiences pain and weakness day after day can have trouble maintaining high spirits. When patients experience setbacks or find their recovery is taking longer than they think it should, they can easily become demoralized. Even someone recovering from the flu can feel discouraged when his knees still wobble 2 weeks after the fever is gone. But discouragement is not major depression. And while periodic feelings of sadness and demoralization go hand in hand with illness, major depression need not.

Because depression can be so elusive, ambiguous, and impressionistic, mental health professionals evaluate it by the number and intensity of symptoms that patients exhibit. Generally they refer to the list of nine symptoms in the American Psychiatric Association's *Diagnostic and Statistical Manual* (DSM-IV) to determine whether a patient is suffering from this disorder. Professional treatment is indicated when physicians see any five of these symptoms lasting for at least two weeks without relief:

1. A persistent sense of hopelessness and disinterest in stimulating activity

2. Loss of interest in normally pleasurable activities, apathy, or loss of sex drive

3. Significant change in appetite patterns, often accompanied by a noticeable change in weight

4. Change in sleep patterns, either insomnia, disrupted sleep, or sleeping more hours than normal

5. Apparent nervous energy or muscle sluggishness

6. Fatigue or lethargy

7. Feelings of inadequacy or guilt

8. Difficulty thinking, concentrating, remembering, or making decisions

9. Preoccupation with death, expressed death wishes, contemplation of or attempts at suicide

Depression and Illness

When patients suffer from prolonged debilitating depression, they do not experience the gains their surgery had promised. Several studies affirm that the number of bypass patients who return to work is lower than expected when age, clinical status, and other relevant factors warrant otherwise. Presumably the problem is depression. One study of heart surgery patients with a good physical outcome revealed that 83% were not employed after surgery and 57% were sexually impaired one to two years later. Too many patients who should feel good are significantly limited in their household and leisure activities. They have problems of low self-esteem, prolonged feelings of gloom, and distorted body image—all symptoms of depression.

This phenomenon is not unique to heart surgery. Studies show that one-third of all surgery patients suffer serious debilitating depression. In part, it comes from feelings of helplessness made worse by feelings that privacy has been invaded and dignity stripped away. This is particularly true of people who pride themselves on their independence and their ability to control the events that shape their lives. When these people need to be fed, bathed, and shaved by someone else, the humility can be unbearable. Parenthetically, surgery patients can also experience depression as a side effect of drugs, notably steroids and some heart and high blood pressure medications.

With illness and surgery of the heart, vulnerability to depression is aggravated by the awesome implications of surgery to this vital organ. More than a pump sending life-bearing oxygen throughout the body, it carries mystical significance as the center of the spirit and soul. Consequently, threats to it and tampering with it carry intensified meaning.

People who suffer heart attacks also encounter depression as a significant complication. After the initial threat of death, many worry that their lives have been permanently altered. Some see their illness as a mark of imperfection or confirmation of their inadequacy, and they lose self-esteem. An estimated 60% of patients suffer from anxiety and depression while they are hospitalized; up to 30% remain depressed for a year following their attack. Some 20% of heart attack patients never return to work, largely because of psychosocial reasons. Moreover, depression can keep people from taking care of themselves. Research in 1995 showed, for example, that when people are depressed they are less likely to take a daily dose of aspirin to help prevent future heart attacks. The authors of this study concluded that depression may affect medical outcome directly by inhibiting compliance with a medical regime.

Depression and illness form a menacing cycle. Illness causes depression, and in turn, depression precedes heart attacks, according to several studies. For people with angina, the correlation is understandable. This crushing pain, which occurs when oxygen is temporarily diminished in the coronary arteries, serves as a constant warning that the heart is not functioning properly. As the pain comes with exercise, eating, or even during rest, it seems to say, ''Be careful. You're vulnerable.'' Thus people with angina exist in a state of vigilance that can create significant psychological stress.

However, a surprising number of patients with no history of angina are also beset with depression before their heart attacks. Dr. Hal Lear, in *Heartsounds*, was one of them. Trapped in a hopeless work situation, he suddenly burst into tears one day while visiting England. Martha Weinman Lear writes: " 'I hate working for them, I hate them all, I hate the whole damned setup,' he had cried, with such an urgent and impotent rage that I should have guessed it might eat like acid into his heart."

Like Hal Lear, 80% of patients participating in one representative study, this one published in 1988, experienced depression during the year before they suffered a heart attack or needed either balloon angioplasty or bypass surgery. Depression correlated with one of these "cardiac endpoints" more than did smoking, elevated cholesterol, high blood pressure, or any other known risk factor. While the researchers acknowledge that their work needs to be replicated and their findings confirmed, they contend that depression seems to be an independent risk factor for heart disease.

After surgery, women encounter depression more frequently than men, some studies suggest. Men and women who need emergency surgery and those who had no disabling angina before surgery seem to have greater difficulty coping with prolonged recuperation than others. Patients whose lives are littered with problems or who encountered numerous changes over the preceding several months also tend to have a harder time. One patient, for example, was the sole provider for her retarded daughter, who had recently been diagnosed as having a chronic kidney problem and dismissed from the residential school she had attended. In addition, the patient expected to be laid off from her job, and she worried how she would support herself in the future. After surgery, she was depressed to the point of wishing she were dead.

"I worry about my daughter. Who will take care of her and who will take care of me? It would be so easy if I could just close my eyes and not wake up," she cried.

Overcoming Depression

Patients who overcome their depression easily often attribute their success to good marriages or supportive, perceptive friends. For other patients, the best therapy is going back to work. One patient, who went into his bypass surgery expecting to die and suffered periodic feelings of intense depression for weeks afterward, believes that going back to work saved his sanity. Many echo this belief. For people who do not work outside the home, putting structure into household work, becoming involved in leisure pursuits, and planning activities with friends offer valuable distractions. Simply breaking the preoccupation with themselves and their bodies often does the trick.

While some depression following surgery is normal and not dangerous, it can become dangerous if it lingers and intensifies. And sometimes, despite monumental efforts to cope effectively, people cannot hold the floodgates of depression secure. The torrent is simply overpowering.

If you lose interest in your favorite activities, take heed. If bad days turn into bad weeks and if these bad weeks are characterized by five of the nine classic symptoms listed earlier in this chapter, you should seek professional help. Turning to a counselor does not imply that you are inadequate or that you have failed in any way. Nor does it suggest that you must spend years in therapy or relinquish control over yourself.

On the contrary, you maintain control because you choose your therapist, who can be a psychologist, psychiatrist, social worker, or member of the clergy. If you are dissatisfied with your choice, you can change. And with the right professional, short-term counseling can be strikingly effective. Likewise, family counseling is often helpful since depression can be as troubling to your family as it is to you. If nothing else, professional intervention permits someone who is not personally involved with you or your family to look at your situation from a new perspective.

To overcome depression, you may need the help of anti-depressant drugs for a few months. Again, this is not a sign of bad attitude, ineffective coping, or failure of any other kind. As the next chapter fully explains, depression may result from change in the biochemical harmony in the brain related to intense stress. If the problem is in fact biochemical in origin, using chemicals to correct it makes sense. Although antidepressants require the careful supervision of a physician, they are safe drugs that impose few side effects.

Think of antidepressants as keys on a key ring. There are many, and each is somewhat unique. Before you find the right fit, you may have to try several different drugs and a variety of dosages. When you hit upon the right formula, your sleep will improve almost immediately. In about 2 weeks, you will find yourself noticeably less depressed, and side effects such as dry mouth and constipation will be minimal. Within 3 to 6 months, antidepressants can usually reverse the chemical imbalance that perpetuated your depression. The new balance should remain stable after you stop taking the medication.

Whether you shed your depression with or without help, the weights do lift. The tears dry up, the anger fades, and the sun comes out.

Points to Remember

❑ Reactive depression, much like grief, is usually self-limiting and not dangerous.

❑ In mild cases, social support, returning to work, and becoming involved in other activities are often effective antidotes.

❑ Worrisome depression is measured by the number and duration of its symptoms.

❏ When it is intense, depression forms a menacing cycle with illness and demands professional care.

❏ Brief treatment with antidepressants can help depression by altering the biochemical balance in the brain.

Chapter Ten

PROMOTING RECOVERY AND GOOD HEALTH

It is easy to understand how patients might encounter infection after heart surgery. Arrhythmias, blood clots, and a host of other complications also seem plausible. But depression? To assert that depression can erupt as a complication of a physical trauma is to accept the integral connection between mind and body.

Hardly new to medical theory, this connection was first acknowledged nearly 5,000 years ago by Huang Ti, the Yellow Emperor of China, who perceived illness as a by-product of frustration. Twenty-five hundred years later, Hippocrates argued that change brings on illness. The mind–body association, central to primitive theories of medicine, lost credence in modern times. But today, solid scientific evidence demonstrates that physical illness and emotional conditions are tightly tied together. Perhaps the most familiar affirmation of this connection is the Type A personality.

Type A Personality

This profile began to emerge in the late 1950s, when California cardiologists Meyer Friedman and Ray Rosenman first observed how quickly the front edges of their waiting room chairs were wearing out. So restive were their patients, the cardiologists reasoned, that they perched at the edge of their seats ready to pounce forward the moment their names were called.

From this observation came the now-familiar personality profile. To a larger degree, Type As are the successful men and women in our society. They are ambitious and aggressive, competitive and hard-driving. They eat fast and play hard. Frequent interruptions anger them, and they rarely take time to unwind. Instead they use every minute to get ahead. They make plans while they shower and read while they eat. They hate waiting in line, and when they are in the car, heaven help the driver who slows down in front of them.

As evidence mounted, it became increasingly clear that the hostility and competitiveness characteristic of people with Type A personalities raised their risk of heart disease. Research also documented that reducing Type A tendencies improved cardiovascular functioning: When business people changed their behavior, they lowered their blood pressure and cholesterol levels. Similarly, heart attack victims who learned to modify their Type A tendencies suffered fewer subsequent heart attacks than patients who did not.

By 1982, the evidence supporting the correlation between Type A personalities and cardiovascular risk was so strong that the National Heart, Lung, and Blood Institute issued an official statement about it:

> The review panel accepts the available body of scientific evidence that Type A behavior . . . is associated with increased risk of clinically apparent coronary heart disease in employed, middle-aged, U.S. citizens. The risk is greater than that imposed by age, elevated . . . blood pressure . . . cholesterol, and smoking, and appears to be in the same order of magnitude as the relative risk associated with the latter of these three factors.

In the ensuing years, however, additional research has reopened the issue. Recent studies have shown, for example, that some people with Type A personalities appear unusually stressed when they are forced to slow down. Moreover, while competitiveness and ambition have been classically viewed as Type A characteristics, new research suggests that workers are most vulnerable if their jobs impose significant pressure but little opportunity to control it. When men and women find their work challenging and rewarding, they are less likely to encounter distress, no matter how hard they work or how high on the corporate ladder they climb.

The exact correlation between Type A tendencies and heart disease appears to be less clear-cut than once was thought. While the concept as a whole may still be evolving, one component, namely the pernicious role of stress, has been apparent throughout. It is stress caused by impatience, frustration, unrelieved anger and other such disquieting emotions that aggravates the physiological conditions compatible with heart disease.

The Theory of Stress

These findings are consistent with the first observations correlating stress and physiological changes, which Hans Selye, M.D., Ph.D., made more than half a century ago. In 1926, Selye, the founder and long-time president of the International Institute of Stress, noticed that when laboratory rats were exposed to stress, their adrenal glands enlarged, organs of their immune system shrank, and the animals developed peptic ulcers. Subsequently, experts learned that when people and other animals are in a state of stress, their blood reveals elevated levels of certain hormones, collectively labeled stress hormones, which suppress immunity to illness and endanger various body systems.

How, one might ask, do emotional reactions, which ostensibly take place in the brain, cause changes in hormones, blood, and the functioning of various organs? Truthfully, no one knows for sure. However, numerous studies support a widely accepted theory.

The theory begins with the discovery that thoughts, attitudes, and convictions are correlated with electrochemical events in the brain. Positron emission tomography (PET), which images the metabolism of the brain, can show the brain in action and documents that as mental or cognitive processes change, cerebral blood flow, physiology, and hormonal balance also change. Integral to these electrochemical events are chemical messengers responsible for relaying electrical impulses throughout the nervous system. These messengers are called neurotransmitters.

Neurotransmitters are produced in the brain. They transmit electrical activity within the brain as well as to all other parts of the body. Some of these stimulate glands to secrete hormones, which enter the blood stream and affect all parts of the body, including the immune system, the cardiovascular system, and the brain. Thus, when someone is frightened, neurotransmitters begin a chain reaction that causes him to sweat, his eyes to widen, and his heart rate to increase.

The hormones and neurotransmitters that connect thoughts and emotions to physiological events work as a two-way street. Emotions can trigger an array of physiological occurrences, as the relationship between Type A personality and heart disease illustrates. Conversely, physiological events can alter emotions. When athletes work out, for example, they experience a rush of certain neurotransmitters called endorphins, which are thought to bring on the "runner's high." Because of the resulting sense of well-being, exercise enthusiasts find that their workouts do as much for the spirit as for the body.

In general, it appears that positive emotions promote good health, and vice versa; also that negative emotions promote illness, and vice versa. Moreover, whether emotions are positive or negative depends more on an individual's perception than on an objective analysis of the event which prompted the feelings. Let's look at these factors one at a time.

Positive Emotions and Good Health

There is increasing evidence that positive emotions strengthen the immune system and thereby promote good health. Harvard psychologist David McClelland discovered that feelings of love and caring increase the body's production of antibodies that fight upper respiratory viruses. Research at the Menninger Clinic suggests that romantic love

Laughter too has been associated with healing.

increases immunity to colds. Romantic love also appears to decrease lactic acid and increase endorphins. These biochemical changes help to explain the vigorous euphoric feelings that often characterize people in love. Faith also seems to promote recovery. A study of patients facing eye surgery revealed that those who expressed trust in their surgeons and their ability to recover healed faster than more skeptical patients. Laughter too has been associated with healing. Since renowned author Norman Cousins first advocated laughter to catalyze recovery in *Anatomy of an Illness as Perceived by the Patient,* several studies have confirmed the healthy physiological effects of humor. People with good senses of humor exhibit elevated levels of antibodies that protect against colds. Similarly, good moods coincide with the suppression of stress hormones and the elevation of endorphins. So convincing is the therapeutic benefit of laughter that several hospitals have established humor centers. For example, St. Joseph's Hospital in Houston has established the "Living Room" for cancer patients. Equipped with audio and video cassette recorders, the space is a haven for patients to watch comedies and listen to their favorite music.

Negative Emotions and Illness

Just as feelings of love, optimism, faith, and humor seem to promote well-being, so pervasive feelings of pessimism, anxiety, frustration, conflict, and stress appear to catalyze a variety of illnesses. For example, Harvard Medical School pediatricians observed that among children whose throat cultures tested positive for strep infections, only those who experienced stress were likely to become ill. Similarly, army recruits who developed upper respiratory infections also showed elevated blood levels of stress hormones. And the blood tests of college students who came down with acute infectious diseases revealed a rise in stress hormones before they began to feel sick. Elevated stress hormones are associated with cold sores, migraine headaches, and ulcers. And they can also promote cholesterol buildup and atherosclerosis, a sequence that helps to explain heart disease and Type A personalities.

Perhaps the most potent correlation between negative emotions and ill health is the excessive rate of illness and death among the bereaved. In Australia, the death rate among new widows rose 3 to 12 times that of their married counterparts. And in England, the death rate for widowers over 54 years of age jumped more than 40% in the first 6 months after the death of their wives. People in grief, like those who suffer from depression, experience weakened immunity to infection as well as a tendency to other physiological difficulties.

These findings coincide with the prevailing theory about how negative emotions alter neurotransmitters and the hormones they affect. Apparently, chronic intense stress, pessimism, and other emotions characteristic of depression affect the brain by depleting the neurotransmitters norepinephrine and dopamine. Moreover, it appears that norepinephrine, dopamine, and a third neurotransmitter, serotonin, play key roles in depression. When optimum amounts of these neurotransmitters fail to travel along the cells in the nervous system, particularly in the front of the brain, the biochemical stage is set for depression. Sleep, appetite, and sex are disrupted. So are moods, movement, motivation, and responsiveness. Even facial expression is altered as depression inhibits control of the muscles around the mouth causing the corners of the mouth to droop.

Several kinds of evidence appear to validate this theory. One, PET scanning reveals that the brain looks different during depression than it does normally. Two, mood-elevating drugs commonly used to treat depression, such as Elavil (Merck Sharp & Dohme [amitriptyline HCI, MSD USP]) and Tofranil (Geigy [imipramine hydrochloride USP]) work by altering the chemical composition of the brain.

Stress, illness, and depression can form a destructive cycle, but they don't have to. The key to breaking the cycle is perception. When people perceive potential stress as distressing, they increase their vulnerability. If they perceive the potential stress as benign, they do not. Thus, a workload that is overwhelming to one person can seem challenging and stimulating to another. As Harvard University's crisis intervention specialist Gerald Caplan observed, when people feel that stress is unmanageable, they begin to feel helpless, and they become vulnerable to depression and illness.

If people can marshal their best coping strategies, they stand the best chance to keep stress in check and thereby prevent the onset of the destructive cycle. This is not to say that people can control the fate of their bodies by improving their attitudes. Attitude, perception, and faith are only part of a large and complex system including genetics, environment, and other factors over which one has no control. Thus, people who assume full responsibility for their well-being and who imply that, with proper effort, they can achieve immortality, are wrong.

Somewhere between the absurdity that death is optional and the misconception that fate is entirely predestined lies the notion that when people cope effectively, they defuse their distress and enhance their well-being. People can usually reduce their stress when they rely on comfortable coping strategies and adapt these strategies to meet the specific demands of the challenge at hand. Let's take another look at some of the patients we discussed earlier in the book and review ways they adapted their coping styles to manage heart surgery.

Coping Effectively

Jacques Monteil, the 55-year-old accountant whose experience we quoted from time to time, has an insistent need to intellectualize his stress. By taking an active role in his health care from the moment he first experienced angina, he was able to manage stress without distress. Thus, he began to keep a diary:

> I had always been concerned about my heart, partly because of my family history of heart disease and partly because I have always found the heart particularly intriguing. This thing that moves inside us, without dependence or apparent dependence on our will, is really unique in the human body. And to know that our life depends on the continuity of that movement adds to the awe with which we look upon the heart.

After suffering for years from angina controlled by medication, Mr. Monteil agreed to have an angiogram, again, ostensibly, out of intellectual drive. "My angina was now at least 6 years old and . . . one had to know exactly what I had," he wrote in his diary. "No other means of investigation so far are as accurate and complete as a film."

Although the angiogram showed several severe blockages, he would not take the recommendation of his cardiologist before he consulted with two others and weighed their opinions. Once he decided upon surgery and selected a hospital and surgeon, he set out to prepare for surgery. He rested, lost weight, and exercised dutifully. He read *Open Heart Surgery* by Ina Yalof because "the main source of apprehension and fear is ignorance and surprise, and this book helped to eliminate both."

After arriving at the hospital, Mr. Monteil met with his surgeon and made some last-minute preparations for his operation. The entry in his diary reads:

> We had a long talk and he impressed me as knowing my file, my history, and my angiogram very thoroughly. . . . He told me what tests would be done. . . . I knew most of this from the book—no surprise.
>
> From my conversations with others who had been operated on, I discovered that many could hear the doctors speak among themselves in spite of the anesthesia and that these conversations later haunted them in their dreams. I decided to put cotton wool

in my ears to avoid this risk. Furthermore, I did not go to sleep too early on the day before surgery so as to be still half asleep at the time the medication was given to me the day of the operation.

By taking such monumental control, Jacques Monteil set himself up to minimize his distress, and for him it worked. He recovered with record speed and 5 years after his surgery was healthy, vigorous, and busy pursuing his career.

In contrast, James Nicholson, whose experiences also appear elsewhere in this text, is much less comfortable assuming responsibility for his care. A mild-mannered, agreeable person who quickly defers to others, he tends to be a quiet worrior. In the stress of impending surgery, he found too much information overwhelming and confusing. He could not find comfort in reading a book on heart surgery or talking to every former patient he encountered. He coped better with small amounts of information repeated often and wrapped in reassurance and encouragement. Thus he filtered out a lot of the information that came his way, and he responded well to comments like, "You'll do just fine." For him, the easiest time was in the ICU; there his natural inclination to dependency was welcomed, and he derived great comfort from the diligent attention of his nurses.

Although everyone has favorite coping strategies, certain strategies are inappropriate in some circumstances. In such instances, the strategy must be modified. For example, since patients come through the earliest postoperative period best when they can depend utterly on their caregivers, patients like Jacques Monteil must modify their instinctive preference for control. These patients often minimize distress by turning their need to control inward. It is patients in this group who are most likely to practice relaxation exercises and self-hypnosis. Since these techniques work best when they have been well practiced, patients whose surgery is elective sometimes practice daily for several weeks. In contrast, people like James Nicholson, who feel comfortable in the dependent role of the ICU patient, often have trouble motivating themselves to take charge of the work inherent in convalescence. These patients can approach advanced recuperation by dutifully obeying orders. When patients effectively adapt their coping strategies to meet the demands of their hospitalization, they come through the experience with a minimum of distress.

Sometimes, people think they are coping well but their behavior belies their perceptions. Such was the case of Paul Stevens, discussed in chapter 5. Mr. Stevens, who had always been easy-going and reasonable, began having temper tantrums soon after he was moved from the ICU. Though he was not aware he was frightened, his fears were ravaging him. Luckily, his nurse recognized his signals of distress and dealt with them appropriately. When patients persistently behave in a strikingly unusual manner, their ability to cope may be disintegrating and crisis intervention may be helpful.

Positive Attitude

While coping styles vary among people, certain characteristics appear in all effective coping strategies. Chief among those qualities is a positive attitude. For some, that translates into faith. For others, it's seeing the proverbial glass as half full rather than half empty. For still others, it's choosing to overlook the downside.

"A person at all times has a choice as to what to focus on, foreground or background, good or bad," research psychiatrist Joel Dimsdale observed.

Trying to keep a positive attitude toward surgery helped Michael Strickland, a patient described in chapter 3, suppress the fear that sometimes threatened to choke him. "The worst times were at night, when I would lie in bed and feel so panicky. Then I'd just say to myself: Strickland, less than three people in a hundred die from this surgery. You're having the operation because the doctor thinks you're strong enough to do well. You will survive. You will recover. And you will be stronger and healthier than you are now.''

Strickland recalled the hypnotic effect the short sentences had on him. He repeated over and over, ''You will survive. You will recover.'' Somehow, miraculously, the anxiety subsided for the moment.

Repeating positive statements is a valuable exercise. It can affect the neurochemicals in the brain and begin the chain that promotes well-being. These statements rarely eradicate negative feelings like worry and disbelief. Rather, they offset them and help to put them in perspective.

You can also enhance your sense of well-being by looking at the positive side of your hospitalization, since it is the perception of events, not the events themselves, that creates stress. Hospitalization does have some positive aspects, after all. It may provide a welcome visit from loved ones who live far away. It can be a respite from household chores and an unhurried opportunity to read a good book and listen to some favorite music. Journalist Douglass Cater, who wrote about his surgery in the *New York Times Magazine,* adopted this attitude. He wrote:

> I have come to treasure the solitude and almost resent the solicitous interruptions of friends and loved ones. . . . For the first time ever, I have the chance to listen to the same movement [of his favorite Prokofiev, Mozart, and Brahms tapes] over and over again. It has a hypnotic effect, especially during those post-midnight hours when the clock always seems to get stuck.

Social Support

While social support is invaluable, the kind of support which patients find helpful varies among individuals. Some patients say the best support comes from other patients. Before surgery, they were encouraged when they heard the tales and saw the scars of people who had been to the operating room before them. Fortunately, many former patients find it therapeutic to counsel newcomers to the hospital. Some hospitals also arrange for prospective patients to meet each other in patient education classes and foster communication among them throughout the hospital experience. Peer support groups in cities throughout the country meet this need as well.

While families and close friends offer valuable support to many patients, some, facing severe threats to health, find that support from the people they love most magnifies their sense of incapacity and lowers their self-esteem. These people might do better with support from other patients and health professionals than with sympathetic attention from friends and family. Others need time alone to resolve emotional distress. One patient, for example, dealt with the incessant irritability he felt for months after surgery by going off by himself for a few days. In the mountains, he was able to defuse his anger, and then he returned to his family.

Given the mounting evidence supporting the interaction of the mind and the body, we feel confident that psychological attitudes can affect recovery. The way people cope with surgery does make a difference. Good coping, in one way or another, incorporates sound social support and a positive attitude. When people inject these qualities into their most comfortable coping styles, they enhance their emotional environment and the biochemical foundation that supports it. More than reducing their vulnerability to depression, they boost their recovery from illness and help promote ongoing good health.

Points to Remember

❑ Thoughts and emotions are related to electrochemical events that connect the mind and the body.

❑ Love, faith, and other positive emotions appear to promote good health while stress and other negative emotions seem to thwart it.

❑ Coping well brings out positive emotions.

❑ Sometimes people must modify their coping strategies to accommodate specific situations.

❑ Constructive coping always incorporates positive attitudes and effective social support.

Chapter Eleven
PRESCRIPTION FOR LIFE

Heart surgery has given you new life. Protect it. Cherish it.

Unfortunately, too many heart surgery patients make impressive resolutions about reforming their lives in the early months after surgery. As their recovery winds down and the whole unsavory experience fades into history, however, they rationalize their way back into the old, bad habits. This is particularly true of people who regularly resort to denial as a coping mechanism. "Oh, I don't have heart disease. I had my plumbing fixed and now I'm fine," they profess as they dig in to their eggs Benedict.

It's a lie, you know. If you had surgery because your coronary arteries were obstructed, you will always have heart disease. The agents that clogged your coronary arteries before surgery will continue to deposit plaque on your native arteries as well as your bypasses. But living prudently is likely to slow the process. So, please, continue to take care of yourself.

Reducing Risk

As you probably know, a number of risk factors increase vulnerability to heart disease, and the more successfully these risk factors stay under control, the less likely your heart disease is to progress. Although age, genetic predisposition, and male gender are beyond anyone's control, high blood pressure, high cholesterol, obesity, diabetes, sedentary life-style, smoking, formation of blood clots, and stress all yield to good management. Just by eating well, exercising regularly, and not smoking you can have a powerful impact on your blood pressure, blood cholesterol, diabetes, and obesity. If you stay away from cigarettes, use aspirin prophylactically, take hormone replacement therapy if you are female, and keep your stress under control, you can take a giant stride forward in protecting your health.

Eating Healthfully

According to the American Heart Association and the National Cholesterol Education Program, a healthy diet contains no more than 30% fat, 10% of which comes from saturated fat. But if you ask the policy makers at either of these organizations, they will readily admit that these recommendations are compromises. They were adopted only because they were considered modest enough for large segments of the population to comply with them. The policy makers will also acknowledge that, although following these guidelines might protect the health of people not threatened by atherosclerosis, it won't do much for those with established disease. Separately, research by California cardiologist Dean Ornish demonstrated that a 30% fat diet might slow the progression of atherosclerosis, but that a diet of 10% fat, together with regular exercise and stress control, has the potential to halt it, even to turn it around. While a diet of only 10% fat is stringent and difficult to maintain, you will do yourself a real favor by striving for a total fat intake of about 20%.

The typical American diet, comprised of about 40% fat and 8,000 or more milligrams of salt, contributes to high cholesterol, high blood pressure, diabetes, and obesity, all independent risk factors for heart disease. Just cutting back on animal protein and visible fats (butter, oil, mayonnaise, etc.) and eating more fruits, vegetables, and grains can often make a dramatic difference in risk profile. When healthy diet is combined with regular exercise, LDL (bad) cholesterol and blood pressure tend to fall and diabetes often comes under control without medication. As a bonus, many people also discover that unwanted pounds melt away, and mounting research suggests that a healthy life-style provides protection from various kinds of cancer too.

We know how threatening changing your diet can feel, but we are confident that you can make this change success-fully. We'll even help you get started. (See Meal Planning Appendix I, which follows this chapter.)

Staying Away from Cigarettes

If you smoke, you must find a way to stop.

Smoking and heart disease make such incompatible bed-fellows that some surgeons refuse to perform bypass surgery on smokers unless they vow to quit. While smoking does help some people keep their weight down, the habit redis-tributes body fat so that smokers become more vulnerable to heart disease and diabetes. It also raises cholesterol. Worse, the carbon monoxide, cyanide, formaldehyde, and other poisons found in every cigarette, cigar, and pipe bowl work together to strain the entire cardiovascular system. Take a puff or chew a wad of tobacco and within seconds, your pulse rate increases as much as 25 beats a minute, and your blood pressure, both systolic and diastolic, climbs as much as 20 points. The carbon monoxide chokes out oxygen in your blood while the nicotine shrinks your native arteries in half and shuts your bypasses down. For these and other reasons, smokers have 70% more heart attacks than non-smokers. Passive smoke, too, has been proven dangerous.

But snuff out the cigarette, and within half an hour your cardiac risk begins to abate. In just a few days, as the nico-tine leaves your body, your blood pressure begins to drop, your pulse rate slows, coronary spasms subside, and your blood makes room for more oxygen. After 4 months, the oxygen in your blood increases enough to raise your energy level and exercise tolerance 16%. And after 5 years, virtu-ally all the risks associated with smoking turn around.

But you don't need to be told that smoking is harmful. In fact, if you resemble at least 80% of other smokers, you want to quit and have already tried but failed. Kicking the habit is so onerous that although 43 million Americans have done it, few succeeded the first time. It took most former smokers between 4 and 10 attempts. Regardless of the approach that finally worked for them, what everyone shared was motivation: a genuine, deep, and abiding desire to quit.

While you were in the hospital, you passed through the period of nicotine withdrawal without even feeling it. With the physical addiction gone, the next step is to dissociate yourself and your activities from cigarettes. Reorder your daily routines. Identify the activities you associate with smoking and change the way you practice that activity. If, for example, you normally smoke at the table after a meal, instead of lingering at the table, get up and become involved in another activity. If you smoke at your desk while you work, sip some herbal tea instead.

Of the 43 million former smokers, 90% quit on their own and they did it cold turkey. To help you join their ranks, numerous self-help aids are available from the American Heart Association, the American Lung Association, and the American Cancer Society. In addition, there is a raft of books, talking books, audiotapes and videotapes dedicated to the same goal.

If you feel you can't succeed on your own, the American Lung Association, the American Cancer Society, and numerous private organizations, such as Smokenders and Smokers Anonymous, offer group support programs. These will teach you the skills of behavior modification and offer you the encouragement and empathy of peers. To find a suitable program in your area, ask your physician for a referral or check the yellow pages in your phone book under Smoking. Depending on who sponsors the programs, they range in cost from nothing to hundreds of dollars. Ironically, sometimes it is the very cost of tuition that motivates people to succeed. Regardless of the specific motivation, those who do best in these programs tend to be those who have tried to quit on their own and failed.

A small percentage of patients have had long-term success with acupuncture and hypnosis, though these techniques seem to have more impact on the early rather than later stages of the process. Nicotine gum and patches, which furnish nicotine without the harmful chemicals found in tobacco, can also help you manage nicotine withdrawal. If you have tried quitting and failed, using supplemental nicotine and attending a support program may offer you the best shot at success.

Whatever your method, keep trying. If you have quit before and relapsed, try again. Since most permanent quitters needed as many as 10 attempts before they experienced enduring success, you are justified in viewing setbacks not as failure but as part of the process. Try again. And again. You can't succeed if you don't try.

Avoiding Stress

As tension mounts, the human body releases hormones that raise blood pressure and promote atherosclerosis. Because of this correlation with heart disease, you've got to make a lifetime commitment to hold the lid on tension.

Professionals are fond of saying, ''Avoid stressful situations.'' It would be nice if you could, but often you can't. When you feel tension mounting, consciously call on your best coping mechanisms to deal with it. If getting caught in rush hour traffic makes you seethe, get absorbed in the news or a good talk show on the radio. Play a cassette of your favorite music or a talking book. Plan your exercise to help diminish stress as well as stimulate your heart. Weave breaks into your business day. Experiment with yoga and relaxation exercises. Attend a stress management workshop. Investigate behavior modification.

Exercising Regularly

Exercise seems to be a virtual panacea. Regular aerobic exercise lowers resting pulse rate and blood pressure. It reduces total cholesterol and improves the ratio of ''good'' to "bad" cholesterols. It helps prevent and control diabetes and osteoporosis. It boosts dieting efforts by burning additional calories, raising metabolic rate, and reducing hunger. It tempers craving for nicotine and aids in smoking cessation. It helps to clear the lungs and passageways of the toxic effects from passive smoke in the environment. It releases stress while it improves mood and enhances a sense of overall well-being.

While aerobic exercise has been prescribed for most patients after heart attack and heart surgery, patients with particularly weak hearts have traditionally been advised against it. Even this belief has fallen under scrutiny. According to a 1990 article in *The Lancet,* riding an exercise bike helped patients in congestive heart failure by making their muscles work more efficiently and thereby reducing their demand for oxygen. As a result, their hearts had an easier time meeting the muscles' need for oxygen.

In patients whose coronary arteries are blocked, exercise has been shown to help build natural bypasses. These collateral vessels, as they are called, grow around occluded vessels spontaneously in response to the heart's demand for oxygen.

Despite the salutary evidence supporting vigorous aerobic exercise for at least 20 minutes at least three times a week, even the most dedicated exercisers sometimes have to battle with inertia in order to get themselves in gear. And for most people accustomed to sedentary living, no amount of scientific evidence can make exercise palatable.

If you're going to make exercise an enduring component of your life, you've got to find an activity that is enjoyable, convenient, and financially feasible. In the later stages of recovery, talk to your doctor about the kinds of exercise that are appropriate for you, and then begin experimenting. Some people are content with walking and happily increase their speed and distance until they have met their aerobic goals. If you find that walking is boring, experiment with bike riding, swimming, using aerobic machines at a fitness club. Try diversions such as reading or watching television while riding an exercise bike, listening to a tape while walking.

If time is a problem, work exercise into your busy day. Instead of taking the elevator, walk up the stairs to your office. Take a walk at lunch time. Park your car a mile or two from your office and walk the rest of the way. Ride a bicycle to work when the weather permits.

Once you define a program that is tolerable, don't expect to love it. Most people who have always been sedentary find that sweat is an acquired taste. But if you force yourself to stick with a regime you can tolerate, you are likely to feel its salutary effects and become addicted. Sometimes the transformation takes 6 months to a year. Stick with it. Persistence pays.

Vitamin Supplements, Aspirin, Hormone Replacement, and Antibiotics

A number of studies have attested to the protective properties of antioxidant vitamins—especially C and E—normally found in fruits and vegetables. Although some of the studies suggest that taking supplements of these vitamins can protect against heart disease and cancer, the research has not been either consistent or conclusive. We still don't know whether these vitamins really help, whether they help only when consumed in food, and what dose is ideal if, in fact, supplements work. Because most of the evidence in support of antioxidant supplements is impressive, many physicians feel they won't hurt and they might help. Others feel that until the state of the science is more complete, taking supplements is premature and irresponsible. If you are interested in antioxidants, talk to your doctor about whether to take them and how much to take.

Research clearly shows that a small dose of aspirin can help prevent the formation of unwanted blood clots, which can cause a heart attack. At the same time, taking even a small dose of aspirin steadily is not without risk. Talk to your doctor about whether prophylactic aspirin is right for you and how much you should be taking.

For women, hormone replacement therapy, taken indefinitely from the time of menopause on, reduces the risk of heart disease by 50%. Taking estrogen (with progesterone if you still have your uterus) also provides powerful protection against osteoporosis, as well as the other symptoms associated with menopause. Although hormone replacement may also increase the risk of breast cancer slightly and although this treatment is not recommended for all women, for most women with heart disease, the benefits strongly outweigh the risks. If you are past menopause and are not already taking hormone replacement therapy, we urge you to discuss this valuable protection with your doctor.

Under certain circumstances, particularly if you had valve surgery, your heart may be more vulnerable to infection than it used to be. Consequently, you may need to take antibiotics to prevent infection before treatment as simple as having your teeth cleaned. Be sure all your physicians and dentists know about your operation.

Looking Ahead

If you follow an exercise regime and low-fat diet today, you stand a better chance than ever before of managing your heart disease in the future. Should you need them, new drugs promise improved control of risk factors and disease symptoms. Progress in emergency treatment for heart attacks offer unprecedented hope for survival and recovery. And new techniques and technology to tame atherosclerosis all brighten the outlook on cardiovascular disease. But none of this modern technology and pharmacology can replace your responsibility to yourself.

Stick with your new eating habits. Keep exercising—not just for your heart but for the emotional lift it provides. Dedicate yourself to less stress. If you're still working, save

For goodness sake, make time for fun.

time for fishing, walking in the woods, visiting your grand-children. If you're retired, take a course at your local college or become an active volunteer. Read for the blind, tutor some children at a neighborhood school, join an environ-mental clean-up campaign.

Heart surgery gave you a unique opportunity to appreci-ate the fragility of life. We hope that now you will find a way every day to savor its blessing.

MEAL PLANNING: SAMPLE MENU FOR ONE WEEK

A diet compromised of 20% fat is built on a foundation of potatoes, rice, beans, fruits, vegetables and other grains. It includes only small amounts of animal protein, even chicken and fish, most baked goods, and high fat foods such as olives, nuts, and avocados. According to the American Heart Association, we must limit total animal protein (exclusive of nonfat yogurt and skim milk) to a maximum of 6 ounces per day. We must also restrict fats, including those used in cooking and baking, to no more than eight units a day, each unit comprised as follows: 1 teaspoon oil or margarine, 1½ teaspoons oil- or mayonnaise-based salad dressing, 2 teaspoons light mayonnaise. In place of fat and animal protein, we must eat a greater proportion of grains, beans, other vegetables, fruits, and nonfat milk products.

Many patients discover that, when they alter their diets in this fashion, they succeed in losing excess weight without any special effort. It's worth noting, however, that complex carbohydrates do contain calories (even though, gram for gram, they contain fewer calories than fats). No matter where the calories come from, if you consume enough of them, you will not lose weight and may even gain. If you have trouble losing weight, reduce your visible fats to three units a day, eat fewer carbohydrates (starches and fruits), and increase the proportion of vegetables in your daily meal plan.

The following sample menu for one week illustrates that it is possible to modify your diet effectively without sacrificing variety or depriving yourself of the pleasures of eating.

Sunday

Breakfast

½ grapefruit
Buttermilk pancakes (Piscatella, *Choices for a Healthy Heart,* * p. 323) with syrup
Coffee or tea

Lunch

Salad niçoise (omit the egg yolk)
French bread

Snack

Frozen nonfat yogurt

Dinner

East Indian Dirty Rice and Chicken (Fisher & Brown, *Low Cholesterol Gourmet,* * p. 184)
Sliced fresh tomato
Fruit chutney

Snack

Apple-pear sauce (Piscatella, *Choices,* p. 523)

Monday

Breakfast

Orange juice
Oatmeal with cinnamon and raisins

*See Some Additional Resources for full reference.

Skim milk
Coffee or tea

Lunch

Roast turkey sandwich on pita bread with lettuce, tomato, sliced onion, 1½ teaspoons Russian dressing
Carrot sticks

Snack

Skim milk
2 brandy snap cookies (Fisher & Brown, *Low Cholesterol Gourmet,* p. 246)

Dinner

Mixed salad with balsamic vinaigrette
Barbecued or broiled salmon steak seasoned with Chef Paul Prudhomme's Magic Seasoning Blends, Seafood Magic
Brown rice pilaf with mushrooms and onions
Steamed broccoli

Snack

Cold lemon souffle (Piscatella, *Choices,* p. 525)

Tuesday

Breakfast

Cranberry juice
French toast (made with egg substitute and cooked in a nonstick skillet coated with butter-flavored, nonfat spray) with preserves
Coffee or tea

Lunch

Lentil soup
Shallot basil bread (Piscatella, *Choices*, p. 333)
Orange and grapefruit slices

Snack

Angel food cake with fresh or frozen blueberries
(Fisher & Brown, *Low Cholesterol Gourmet*, p. 248)
Herbal tea

Dinner

Linguine with white clam sauce
Baby lettuce salad with endive, raspberry vinaigrette

Snack

Apple

Wednesday

Breakfast

½ banana
Cold cereal of choice
Skim milk
Whole wheat toast with jam
Coffee or tea

Lunch

Vegie-melt sandwich on pita (mushrooms, onions, tomatoes, sprouts, and ½ oz Jarlsberg cheese)
Cucumber spears

Snack

Fresh strawberries

Dinner

Puree of carrot soup
Barbecued or broiled flank steak
Roasted red potatoes
Braised leek, celery, and zucchini

Snack

Chocolate pudding (Piscatella, *Choices*, p. 531)

Thursday

Breakfast

Mixed fruit and nonfat yogurt garnished with wheat germ
Oatmeal toast with jam

Lunch

Tuna-stuffed tomato (mixed with 2 tsp. low-fat mayonnaise
and nonfat yogurt to taste)
Lettuce, cucumber slices, carrot sticks
French bread

Snack

Baked taco chips (soft tortillas sprayed with Pam and baked
at 350° for 10 minutes)
Salsa

Dinner

Chicken stir-fry with mixed oriental vegetables
Steamed rice

Snack

> Skim milk
> 2 low-fat cookies (Pepperidge Farm Bordeaux and Ginger Man contain just 3 grams of fat per cookie, for example)

Friday

Breakfast

> Baked apple
> Wheatena with skim milk
> Coffee or tea

Lunch

> Chicken salad (made with 2 tsp. low-fat mayonnaise and nonfat yogurt to taste) on rye, lettuce and tomato slices
> Carrot sticks

Snack

> Fresh or canned pineapple slices

Dinner

> Caesar salad (dressing made with egg substitute)
> Vegetarian lasagne
> Italian bread

Snack

> Rice pudding (Fisher & Brown, *Low Cholesterol Gourmet,* p. 249)

Saturday

Breakfast

Grapefruit juice
Mushroom omelet (Fisher & Brown, *Low Cholesterol Gourmet,* p. 275)
Bagel with apple butter

Lunch

Baked potato topped with chile and garnished with grated cheese

Snack

Creamy banana puree (Piscatella, *Choices,* p. 513)

Dinner

Minestrone (Piscatella, *Choices,* p. 360)
Rosemary baked chicken
Steamed green beans
Bulgur wheat

Snack

Sorbet

SOME ADDITIONAL RESOURCES

AARP Pharmacy Service. (1992). *Prescription Drug Handbook.* (2nd ed.). New York: Harper Perennial. Thorough and easy to understand. Advisory board of 25.

Benson, H., & Klipper, M. Z. (1976). *The Relaxation Response.* New York: Avon Books. The theory and practice of one approach to relaxation.

Blacher, R. S. (1987). *The Psychological Experience of Surgery.* New York: John Wiley. An in-depth discussion designed for medical professionals but no less meaningful to the general public.

Brody, J. (1987). *Jane Brody's Nutrition Book* and *Jane Brody's Good Food Book: Living the High Carbohydrate Way.* New York: Bantam. Information on nutrition with sound tips for converting to a more healthful eating style.

Cousins, N. (1989). *Head First: The Biology of Hope.* New York: E. P. Dutton. A journal recounting 10 years of investigating how positive emotions promote health, by the author of *Anatomy of an Illness as Perceived by the Patient.* Includes a persuasive scientific bibliography.

Dietrich, E. B., & Cohan, C. (1994). *Women and Heart Disease.* New York: Ballatine. A comprehensive discussion of symptoms, diagnosis, treatment and preventive strategies as they apply to women, as well as insights into the research and policy practices responsible for the myth that heart disease afflicts only men.

Fensterheim, H., & Baer, J. (1982). *Stop Running Scared.* New York: Dell. Although this book addresses mental health problems, it offers excellent self-help materials for managing anxiety and fear; these materials are applicable to the heart surgery experience.

Fisher, L., & Brown, W. V. (1988). *Low Cholesterol Gourmet.* Washington, DC: Acropolis Books. This is one of two cookbooks whose recipes are incorporated in the Meal Planning Appendix. This attractively produced volume offers a valuable discussion of cooking methods and available substitutes for forbidden foods. In addition, it includes a wealth of imaginative and tasty recipes, each accompanied by a cholesterol and saturated fat analysis. One caveat: because the authors are sometimes less than precise in their instructions, these recipes will work best in the hands of an experienced cook.

Halperin, J. L., & Levine, R. (1985). *Bypass.* Tucson, AZ: The Body Press. A comprehensive, intellectual discussion of heart disease and heart surgery. The discussion of some of the difficulties surrounding recovery and returning to work is especially good.

Harvard Heart Letter, T. H. Lee & L. Goldman (co-eds.), and *Harvard Health Letter,* W. I. Bennett (ed.). Boston: Harvard Medical School Health Publications Group. Both are published monthly to disseminate and interpret medical news.

Health Letter. S. Wolf (ed.). Washington, DC: The Health Research Group. Published monthly to help consumers make knowledgeable decisions about their health.

Hoffman, N. Y. (1987). *Change of Heart: The Bypass Experience.* New York: Harper & Row. Case histories of bypass patients plus imaginative tips for handling some aspects of the experience.

Horowitz, L. C. (1988). *Taking Charge of Your Medical Fate.* New York: Random House. A discussion of why it is important to participate actively in your medical care and sensible guidance for how to do it.

Levin, R. F. (1989). *Heartmates: A Survival Guide For Cardiac Spouses.* New York: Pocket Books. A detailed guide to coping for the heart patient's spouse. This book describes the spouse's experience in much the same way *Coping with Heart Surgery and Bypassing Depression* describes the patient's.

Mayo Clinic Heart Book. (1993). New York: William Morrow. Ample easy-to-understand book that covers anatomy, physiology, symptom guide, emergency care, life-style recommendations, and a reliable discussion of diagnosis and treatment options.

Moyers, B. (1993). *Healing and the Mind.* Garden City, NY: Doubleday. How the mind affects illness and recovery. A companion book to the PBS series.

Ornish, D. (1992). *Dr. Dean Ornish's Program For Reversing Heart Disease.* New York: Times Books. Half the book offers clear understanding of heart disease, its causes, and the how-to of a healthy life-style. The other half contains tasty, innovative vegetarian recipes.

Ornstein, R., & Sobel, D. (1987). *The Healing Brain.* New York: Simon & Schuster. Contemporary neurological research supporting the mind–body connection to health.

Pimm, J. B., & Feist, J. R. (1984). *Psychological Risks of Coronary Bypass Surgery.* New York: Plenum. A thorough presentation of the study which inspired *Coping with Heart Surgery and Bypassing Depression.*

Piscatella, J. C. (1987). *Choices for a Healthy Heart.* New York: Workman. This is the second of two cookbooks whose recipes are incorporated in the Meal Planning appendix. In addition to over 200 pages of creative recipes, each of which is followed by a complete nutritional analysis, this book offers practical information to help you reduce your cardiac risk. One of the

book's greatest strengths is its lesson on how to interpret misleading food labels and accurately assess how much fat you're
getting.

Raichlen, S. (1992). *High Flavor, Low-Fat Cooking.* Charlotte, VT:
Camden House and (1995) *High Flavor, Low-Fat Vegetarian
Cooking.* New York: Viking. The Rolls-Royce of low-fat cookbooks. The recipes are involved and time-consuming but the
results are fabulous. This is a real treasure for people who love
to cook and love to eat.

Siegel, B. S. (1989). *Peace, Love and Healing.* New York:
Harper & Row. Inspirational guidance for using the mind–body
connection to catalyze recovery.

Simon, H. B. (1994). *New Ways To Live Well Without Drugs or
Surgery.* Boston: Little, Brown. Up-to-date information on diet,
antioxidants, aspirin, estrogen, and more.

Sunshine, L., & Wright, J. W. (1987). *The Best Hospitals in
America.* New York: Henry Holt. A discussion of what makes
a hospital great and an annotated listing of 64 outstanding medical institutions.

Tufts University Diet and Nutrition Letter. S. N. Gershoff (ed.).
Medford, MA: Tufts University School of Nutrition. Published
monthly to disseminate the latest findings on diet and nutrition.

Yalof, I. L. (1983). *Open Heart Surgery.* New York: Random
House. Includes easy-to-understand descriptions of the various
diagnostic tests relevant to heart disease and complications that
can follow surgery.

GLOSSARY

Analgesic: Medications, both narcotic and nonnarcotic, used to quiet pain.

Aneurysm: A bubble or protrusion of a blood vessel or of scarred, nonfunctional heart muscle that catches blood and keeps it from circulating efficiently. Aneurysms are repaired surgically by cutting out the bubble and sewing the resulting hole closed.

Angina: Chest pain caused by the temporary constriction of a coronary artery and insufficiency of blood delivered to the heart muscle. Sometimes pain caused by this insufficiency is felt in the left shoulder, left arm, and jaw. Pain similar to indigestion can also occur.

Angiogram: See CARDIAC CATHETERIZATION.

Anticipatory Guidance: Information provided before an experience, including details about the events, sensations, and emotions that are likely to occur.

Anticoagulant: A drug, such as coumadin or heparin, which retards blood clotting.

Anti-inflammatory: Counteracting or suppressing inflammation. Also a drug, such as aspirin, ibuprofen, indomycin, or cortisone, which counteracts or suppresses the inflammatory process.

Anxiety: A pervasive feeling of dread, apprehension, and impending disaster. It can cause muscles to become tense, breathing to become faster, and the heart to beat more rapidly.

Aorta: The main trunk of the artery system. The aorta sends freshly oxygenated blood from the heart to the lesser arteries, which in turn deliver it throughout the body. When vein grafts are used for bypass, one end of each graft is connected to the aorta. The other end is connected to the occluded coronary artery below the point of blockage.

Aortic valve: The valve that separates the left ventricle from the aorta. When this ventricle contracts, the valve opens and releases blood into the ascending aorta. When the ventricle relaxes, the valve closes and prevents the blood in the aorta from sliding back into the ventricle. Because this valve controls the passage of freshly oxygenated blood into the arterial system, this is probably the most important of the four valves.

Arrhythmia: Sometimes called palpitations. An irregular or abnormal heartbeat.

Artery: A blood vessel that carries blood from the heart to another part of the body.

Ascending Aorta: The part of the aorta closest to the left ventricle. This huge vessel, 1-inch in diameter, handles blood rich with oxygen and feeds the coronary arteries.

Atherosclerosis: The condition in which plaque builds up within the arteries. As a result of atherosclerosis, arteries harden and narrow. The resulting disease is also called arteriosclerosis, or hardening of the arteries.

Atrial–septal defect: A hole in the wall separating the right atrium from the left. This defect causes oxygen-rich blood, which has just entered the left atrium from the lungs, to mix with oxygen-depleted blood in the right atrium. To compound the problem, some of the blood never gets out into the body. Instead, it goes round and round from the left atrium to the right atrium to the right ventricle into the lungs and back into the left atrium. To compensate, the heart must work several times as hard as it should. The defect can be repaired surgically.

Autoimmune response: The phenomenon by which the body's immune system attacks its own tissues. This sometimes occurs as

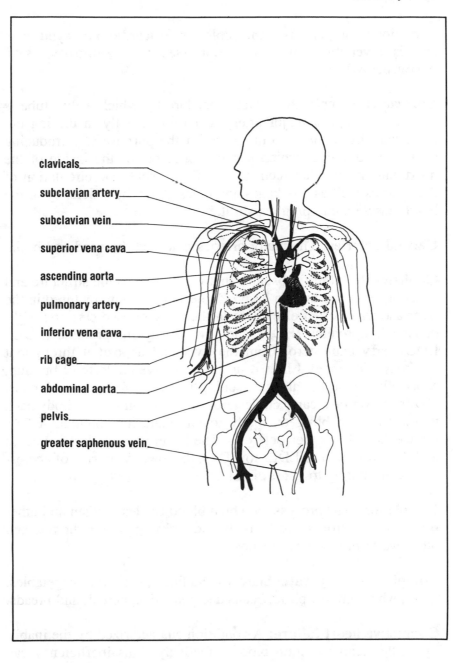

clavicals

subclavian artery

subclavian vein

superior vena cava

ascending aorta

pulmonary artery

inferior vena cava

rib cage

abdominal aorta

pelvis

greater saphenous vein

a reaction to surgery, is responsible for postcardiotomy syndrome, and is reversible with medication (see POSTCARDIOTOMY SYNDROME below).

Cardiac catheterization: The procedure by which a thin tube is threaded through a major artery and vein (usually in the leg but sometimes in the arm) to the heart for the purpose of introducing a radio-opaque dye, which permits an X ray of the inside of the heart and arteries that feed it. This film reveals the circulation of the heart as well as blockages and clues about the efficiency of the heart muscle's pumping capabilities.

Carotid arteries: The major arteries that feed the head and brain.

Cholesterol: A fatty substance that is essential to the structure and functioning of the human body. Cholesterol is manufactured in the liver and transported elsewhere in the body by two carriers: high-density lipoproteins (HDL) and low-density lipoproteins (LDL). LDLs carry cholesterol from the liver and deposit it throughout the body. Too many LDLs result in excessive cholesterol buildup, especially inside the arteries, setting the stage for atherosclerosis. HDLs, in contrast, carry cholesterol from throughout the body back to the liver, enabling the body to eliminate it. Abundant HDLs reduce the risk of atherosclerosis. The lower your cholesterol count and the proportion of LDLs to HDLs, the lower your risk of cholesterol contributing to heart disease.

Circulation: The process by which blood carries oxygen and other fuels to cells throughout the body and picks up carbon dioxide and other waste products for disposal.

Complex carbohydrate: Starches and fibers, including vegetables, fruits, whole grains, pasta, beans and peas, rice, cereal, and breads.

Congestive heart failure: A condition characterized by the inability of the heart to pump blood effectively. This inefficiency can cause the blood to back up into the lungs. It can also cause decreased production of urine and retention of fluid in the lungs, abdomen, and legs. The condition is treated with digitalis to improve the heart's pumping capacity and diuretics to rid the body of excess fluid. Symptoms of congestive heart failure sometimes occur after heart surgery because of the surplus of fluids pumped into the body during the operation.

Coping: The schemes and strategies people may employ in response to stress. While coping, in the vernacular, implies success, the denotation of the term does not. Thus, breaking down a large problem into manageable components is a coping strategy, and often a successful one. But, technically speaking, smoking and nail biting are coping strategies as well.

Coronary: Also called a heart attack or myocardial infarction. It refers to the occlusion of a coronary artery from a blood clot or atherosclerotic debris and results in the death of part of the heart muscle. During the healing process, scar tissue forms in the area of damage. Recent medical advances can reduce muscle damage if treatment is instituted immediately.

Coronary arteries: The first branches off the ascending aorta, which feed fresh blood to the muscle of the heart. Confusion about circulation often occurs because the heart pumps blood throughout the body but also needs blood for its own nourishment. This circulation is managed by the two coronary arteries and their branches. The right coronary artery and its subsidiaries feed the right atrium and the right ventricle, which sends blood to the lungs to be replenished with oxygen. The all-important left main artery feeds the powerful left side of the heart. The left atrium, which receives oxygenated blood from the lungs, is fed by some branches of the left circumflex artery. Because the pumping capability of the left ventricle is integral to the efficiency with which the blood is delivered throughout the body, unobstructed blood flow through the left main coronary artery and its primary branches is particularly important.

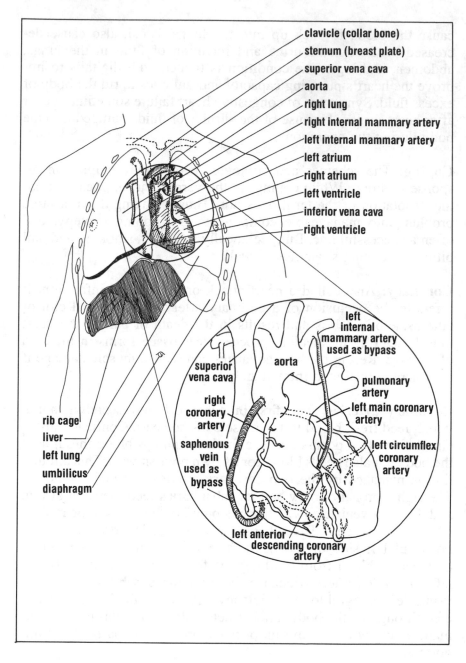

clavicle (collar bone)
sternum (breast plate)
superior vena cava
aorta
right lung
right internal mammary artery
left internal mammary artery
left atrium
right atrium
left ventricle
inferior vena cava
right ventricle

rib cage
liver
left lung
umbilicus
diaphragm

left internal mammary artery used as bypass

superior vena cava
aorta
right coronary artery
pulmonary artery
left main coronary artery
saphenous vein used as bypass
left circumflex coronary artery

left anterior descending coronary artery

Crisis: A situation or event that produces stress. During crisis, people stop functioning in their usual ways. They become overwhelmed and feel anxious. They have trouble solving problems and setting priorities, and, as a result, feel helpless.

Crisis intervention: Short-term counseling specially designed to help people solve the problems which seem insurmountable in the context of crisis. This therapy incorporates anticipatory guidance, problem solving, conceptual information, and the encouragement of social support. Although crises usually aggravate other existing problems, crisis intervention does not deal with those problems. Its goal is to return the person in crisis to his or her precrisis state.

Denial: The conscious or unconscious refusal to accept the existence of anxiety-producing events, ideas, or feelings.

Depression: A psychological state often characterized by some combination of the following: dejected mood, disinterest in normally stimulating activities, sleep and appetite disturbances, low energy, difficulties thinking and concentrating, feelings of inadequacy and guilt, and medical complaints.

Diuretic: A drug, such as Lasix (Hoechst-Roussel [furosemide]), which rids the body of excess fluid and sodium.

Edema: Swelling caused by excessive fluid in the body.

Electrocardiogram (EKG): A graphic representation of the electric current produced by the heart.

Electrolytes: Chemicals including sodium, potassium, chlorides, bicarbonates, calcium, and magnesium which exist in a dissolved state in the blood and other body fluids. In order for the body to function properly and for a person to feel well, electrolytes must be properly balanced. Surgery may prompt a temporary imbalance, which can trigger an array of uncomfortable but correctable symptoms.

Endocardium: The membrane that lines the inside of the heart. An inflammation of this membrane, called *subacute bacterial endocarditis,* can weaken the aortic valve and prompt the need for surgery to replace it.

Femoral artery: One of the main arteries of the leg located near the groin. This is the artery usually entered for cardiac catheterization, though the brachial artery, located on the inner side of the arm, is sometimes used.

Fibrillation: Erratic electrical activity of the heart. Atrial fibrillation, or erratic electrical activity of the upper chambers, causes irregular contraction of the lower chamber and palpitations, characterized by the feeling of galloping horses. Although palpitations can be disconcerting, atrial fibrillation is generally not a serious condition. Ventricular fibrillation, in contrast, results in inefficient pumping of the lower chamber and can cause death if it is not treated immediately.

Heart-lung machine: The mechanical device that exchanges carbon dioxide for oxygen in the blood and pumps reoxygenated blood through the body while the heart is stopped during surgery.

Intubate: To insert a tube between the vocal cords and into the windpipe. The other end of this tube is connected to a respirator, which controls breathing for patients during surgery and for several hours afterward.

Left main coronary artery: The source of fresh blood to the entire left side of the heart (see definition for CORONARY ARTERIES above). Blockage of this artery is a dire threat to life.

Left ventricle: The very muscular chamber of the heart that pumps freshly oxygenated blood throughout the body (see definition for CIRCULATION above).

Mammary arteries: The two arteries running alongside the breast plate (sternum). These internal thoracic arteries, as they are also called, feed the chest wall. They are expendable, however, and are often used for bypass grafts. The mammary artery takes longer to prepare for use as a graft, but it is likely to remain unclogged for a greater number of years than the saphenous vein, the other vessel commonly used for bypass.

Mitral valve: The valve that separates the two chambers on the left side of the heart. This two-part valve derives its name from a bishop's headpiece (called a miter), which it resembles. The valve, sometimes also called a parachute valve because it is attached to a supporting ring by two long shrouds, permits blood to fall from the left atrium into the ventricle when the atrium contracts. When the atrium relaxes, the valve closes to prevent the blood from backing up into the atrium and, from there, into the lungs. Next to the aortic valve, this is the heart's second most important valve.

Myxoma: The most common of heart tumors. Pieces of spongy growth can break off and travel with the blood stream to the brain, where it may cause ministrokes. Or it can clog the mitral valve, preventing efficient passage of oxygenated blood into the left ventricle and, from there, out into the body. This tumor is rarely cancerous, and surgical removal cures the condition permanently.

Neurological difficulties: Any of numerous problems emanating from the brain possibly associated with heart surgery. These range from stroke to transient difficulties concentrating and include numbness, tingling, and weakness in the limbs; speech difficulties; and slowed thinking, confusion, and memory loss. These problems are rarely severe and seldom permanent.

Nitroglycerin: A drug commonly used to treat angina. It is administered by tablet, which is placed under the tongue; long-acting capsule, which is swallowed; or transdermal patch, worn like a Band-Aid on the skin. In an emergency it can be given intravenously. Nitroglycerin dilates the arteries temporarily, thus improving blood flow to the heart and relieving chest pain.

Nuclear scan: A variety of X ray studies incorporating radioisotopes that are injected into the bloodstream, to reveal the functioning of the heart. These tests can accurately measure the efficiency of the heart pump and show areas where the muscle has been injured. While nuclear scans often fit into a thorough diagnostic workup, they cannot take the place of cardiac catheterization because only catheterization can reveal blockages in the coronary arteries.

Oxygenation: The process of infusing blood with oxygen, which takes place in the lungs or, during heart surgery, in the oxygenator of the heart–lung machine.

Pacemaker: An electrical device used to maintain the electric impulse at a desired rate when the heart cannot do so independently. Two thin wires affixed to the heart temporarily during surgery are connected to an external pacemaker, which is often needed to regulate the heartbeat for several days after surgery. When the electrical system of the heart proves to be permanently unreliable, a tiny internal pacemaker can be surgically implanted near the heart under local anesthesia.

Palpitations: See ARRHYTHMIA.

Paranoia: Delusions of persecution. Patients occasionally experience paranoia in the ICU. This is a transient problem experienced most commonly by the elderly and caused, in part, by poor circulation in the brain as a result of enforced bed rest. Once patients are moved to a regular hospital room and spend some time out of bed, these delusions almost always disappear.

Platelet: A type of blood cell critical to the clotting mechanism.

Pleurisy: An inflammation of the membrane which lines the chest cavity accompanied by fluid exuded into the cavity. The condition can occur as a mild complication of heart surgery and is character-ized by pain in the side, a chill, fever, and dry cough. If the condi-tion worsens, pain lessens, but as fluids build up, breathing becomes difficult and the fluid may need to be drained.

Postcardiotomy syndrome: A common complication that can set in during the first weeks after surgery. It is characterized by fever and other flulike symptoms. Chest pain and depression may also occur.

Postpump syndrome: Temporary mental difficulties (e.g., with thinking, remembering, reading, and concentrating) that can occur after heart surgery. These problems appear to be somehow related to the heart–lung machine and ordinarily disappear within a year after surgery.

Projection: A mental mechanism by which people repress emo-tions or attitudes into their subconscious and view them as coming from someone else.

Psychosis: A severe mental disorder. After heart surgery, patients occasionally experience psychosis briefly in the form of paranoia (see also PARANOIA).

Pulmonary valve: The valve separating the right atrium from the blood vessel that leads to the lung. It is a pocket valve, like the aortic valve.

Right atrium: The chamber of the heart that receives blood laden with waste products (see CIRCULATION). While the heart–lung ma-chine is in operation, blood is routed into the machine via a tube inserted into an opening in this chamber.

Saphenous vein: A large, superficial, nonessential vein in the leg that is often used for coronary artery grafts in bypass surgery. There are two saphenous veins in each leg. One runs from the thigh to the foot and the other from the knee to the foot.

Splinting: Supporting the chest by hugging a stiff pillow in order to minimize the pain caused by coughing, sneezing, and other actions that put strain on the incision.

Stenosis: A narrowing or stiffening. Mitral valve stenosis refers to scarring or calcification, which prevents the valve from opening fully and permitting blood to pass through it efficiently. Coronary stenosis refers to atherosclerosis or narrowing caused by a clot, either of which can prevent or slow blood flow.

Stress test: Assessment of the capability of the heart to withstand exercise. The patient confronts increasingly challenging exercise on a treadmill or stationary bicycle while an electrocardiogram traces the electrical activity of the heart and blood pressure is monitored. Sometimes a nuclear scan is coordinated with this study.

Subclavian vein: The large vein at the base of the neck. In preparation for heart surgery, a catheter is threaded through this vein into the heart and then into the pulmonary artery to assess how the right side of the heart is functioning before, during, and after the operation.

Tricuspid valve: The valve that separates the two chambers of the heart. As the name implies, it has three parts and is a parachute valve, like the mitral valve. When the left atrium contracts, this valve opens and permits blood to fall from the atrium into the ventricle.

Vein: A vessel that carries blood from other parts of the body to the heart.

INDEX

ABOUT THE AUTHORS

Carol Cohan, M.A., has written and lectured about health since 1976 and has won awards for her work on magnetic resonance imaging and heart disease in women. She has taught writing at The American University in Washington, D.C. for 10 years, won the university's Outstanding Teaching award, and continued to teach communications seminars for the business community. A gourmet cook as well, Ms. Cohan demonstrates low-fat gourmet cooking and appeared as a regular guest on television's Low Cholesterol Gourmet show. She is a graduate of the University of Maryland and Columbia University, a co-author of *Women and Heart Disease* (Times Books, 1992; Ballantine, 1994), and is presently completing a book about protecting vitality in old age.

June B. Pimm, Ph.D., is a clinical psychologist who has conducted extensive research and published widely in developmental psychology and behavioral medicine. In 1970, she wrote and directed the award winning film "Child Behavior Equals You." Formerly on the faculty at Carlton, she presently holds the title of Associate Professor at the University of Miami School of Medicine, where she teaches and conducts research in behavioral medicine. Dr. Pimm is a graduate of McGill and Carleton universities and co-author of *Psychological Risks of Coronary Bypass Surgery* (Plenum Press, 1984).

James R. Jude, M.D., Board-certified cardiovascular surgeon in private practice in Miami, Florida, graduated from the University of Minnesota School of Medicine and completed his surgical training at Johns Hopkins University. At Hopkins, Dr. Jude developed cardiopulmonary resuscitation (CPR) with William Kouwenhoven and Guy Knickerbocker. Subsequently, he was Chief of Heart and Lung Surgery at the University of Miami School of Medicine, where he remains Clinical Professor of Surgery. Dr. Jude is a Fellow of the American College of Chest Physicians and the American College of Cardiology. He won the American Heart Association Award of Merit for his work on CPR and was awarded the title of Hopkins Scholar by Johns Hopkins University. He has published many scientific articles and is co-author of *Cardiopulmonary Resuscitation*.